David Gray

Poetical Works

A New and Enlarged Edition

David Gray

Poetical Works
A New and Enlarged Edition

ISBN/EAN: 9783337777760

Printed in Europe, USA, Canada, Australia, Japan

Cover: Foto ©Thomas Meinert / pixelio.de

More available books at **www.hansebooks.com**

THE
POETICAL WORKS

OF

DAVID GRAY

A NEW AND ENLARGED EDITION, EDITED BY
HENRY GLASSFORD BELL

Glasgow
JAMES MACLEHOSE
PUBLISHER TO THE UNIVERSITY

LONDON: MACMILLAN AND CO.
1874

TO

The Memory of

HENRY GLASSFORD BELL,

LATE SHERIFF OF LANARKSHIRE,

THIS VOLUME,

ON WHICH HIS LATEST LITERARY LABOUR

WAS BESTOWED,

IS

Affectionately Dedicated.

INTRODUCTORY NOTE.

THIS new Edition of the Works of David Gray, containing, it is believed, all the maturely finished poems of the author, is a double memorial. It commemorates "the thin-spun life" of a man of true genius and rare promise, and the highly cultured judgment and tender sympathies of a critic who has passed away in the vigorous fulness of his years.

A specimen page of "The Luggie," forwarded with an appreciative letter from a friend, reached the author on the day before his death. He received it as "good news"—the fragmentary realization of his ambitious dreams—and, in the hope that his name might not be wholly forgotten, said he could now enter "without tears" into his rest.

Within a week before his removal from amongst us, Mr. Glassford Bell was engaged in correcting the proofs of the present edition. He had selected from a mass of MSS. and other material what new pieces he thought worthy of insertion in this enlarged edition—he had rearranged the whole and finally revised the greater part of the volume, which it was his intention to preface with a Memoir and Criticism. He looked forward to accomplishing this labour of love in a period of retirement from more active work which he had proposed to pass in Italy.

It has been thought inadvisable to commit to other hands the unexpectedly interrupted task. For a statement of the few and simple vicissitudes of the Poet's career, as well as a brief but discriminating estimate of his rank in our literature, the reader is referred to the speech—at the close of the volume—delivered by Mr. Bell, nine years ago, on the inauguration of the Monument in the "Auld Aisle" Burying-ground. Of the movement which resulted in this tribute to departed genius, the late Sheriff was one of the most active promoters. Himself a poet, and a generous patron of all genuine art, the West of Scotland has known no "larger heart" or "kindlier hand." There is something suggestive in the fact that his last effort was to throw another wreath on the early tomb of David Gray.

March, 1874.

CONTENTS.

	PAGE
THE LUGGIE,	1
IN THE SHADOWS,	63
A WINTER RAMBLE,	99
THE HOME-COMER,	104
MY BROWN LITTLE BROTHER OF THREE,	108
THE "AULD AISLE,"	111
TO JEANETTE,	120
THE POET AND HIS FRIEND,	124
THE TWO STREAMS,	127
EVENING,	132
THE LOVE-TRYST,	134
AN EPISTLE TO A FRIEND,	139
A VISION OF VENICE,	145
THE ANEMONE,	150
THE YELLOWHAMMER,	154
THE CUCKOO,	158

CONTENTS.

	PAGE
FAME,	161
HONEYSUCKLE,	164
WHERE THE LILIES USED TO SPRING,	167
SNOW,	170
OCTOBER,	175
THE ROMAN DYKE,	179

Sonnets.

EZEKIEL,	183
THE MAVIS,	184
DESPONDENCY,	185
THE MOON, I., II.,	186
THE LUGGIE, I., II., III.,	188
THOMAS THE RHYMER,	191
THE LIME-TREE,	192
THE BROOKLET,	193
MAIDENHOOD,	194
SLEEP,	195
THE DAYS OF OLD MYTHOLOGY,	196
DISCONTENTMENT,	197
SNOW,	198
THE THRUSH,	199
STARS,	200
MY EPITAPH,	201
GRAY'S MONUMENT,	203

The Luggic.

A

The Luggie.

THAT impulse which all beauty gives the soul
Is languaged as I sing. For fairer stream
Rolled never golden sand unto the sea,
Made sweeter music than the Luggie, gloom'd
By glens whose melody mingles with her own.
The uttered name my inmost being thrills,
A word beyond a charm; and if this lay
Could smoothly flow along and wind to the end
In natural manner, as the Luggie winds
Her tortuous waters, then the world would list
In sweet enthralment, swallowed up and lost,

As he who hears the music that beguiles.

For as the pilgrim on warm summer days

Pacing the dusty highway, when he sees

The limpid silver glide with liquid lapse

Between the emerald banks—with inward throe

Blesses the clear enticement and partakes,

(His hot face meeting its own counterpart

Shadowy, from an unvoyageable sky)

So would the people in these later days

Listen the singing of a country song,

A virelay of harmless homeliness;

These later days, when in most bookish rhymes,

Dear blessed Nature is forgot, and lost

Her simple unelaborate modesty.

And unto thee, my friend! thou prime of soul

'Mong men; I gladly bring my first-born song!

Would it were worthier for thy noble sake,

True poet and true English gentleman!

Thy favours flattered me, thy praise inspired :
Thy utter kindness took my heart, and now
Thy love alleviates my slow decline.

Beneath an ash in beauty tender leaved,
And thro' whose boughs the glimmering sunshine
  flow'd
In rare ethereal jasper, making cool
A chequered shadow in the dark-green grass,
I lay enchanted. At my head there bloomed
A hedge of sweet-brier, fragrant as the breath
Of maid belovëd when her cheek is laid
To yours in downy pressure, soft as sleep.
A bank of harebells, flowers unspeakable
For half-transparent azure, nodding, gleamed
As a faint zephyr, laden with perfume,
Kissed them to motion, gently, with no will.
Before me streams most dear unto my heart,
Sweet Luggie, sylvan Bothlin—fairer twain

Than ever sung themselves into the sea,
Lucid Ægean, gemmed with sacred isles—
Were rolled together in an emerald vale;
And into the severe bright noon, the smoke
In airy circles o'er the sycamores
Upcurled—a lonely little cloud of blue
Above the happy hamlet. Far away,
A gently-rising hill with umbrage clad,
Hazel and glossy birch and silver fir,
Met the keen sky. Oh, in that wood, I know,
The woodruff and the hyacinth are fair
In their own season; with the bilberry
Of dim and misty blue, to childhood dear.
Here, on a sunny August afternoon,
A vision stirred my spirit half-awake
To fling a purer lustre on those fields
That knew my boyish footsteps; and to sing
Thy pastoral beauty, Luggie, into fame.
Now, while the nights are long, by the dear hearth

Of home I write; and ere the mavis trills
His smooth notes from the budding boughs of March,
While the red windy morning o'er the east
Widens, or while the lowly sky of eve
Burns like a topaz;—all the dear design
May reach completion, married to my song
As far as words can syllable desire.

May yet the inspiration and delight
That proved my soul on that Autumnal day,
Be with me now, while o'er the naked earth
Hushfully falls the soft, white, windless snow!

Once more, O God, once more before I die,
Before blind darkness and the wormy grave
Contain me, and my memory fades away
Like a sweet-coloured evening, slowly sad—
Once more, O God, thy wonders take my soul.
A winter day! the feather-silent snow

Thickens the air with strange delight, and lays
A fairy carpet on the barren lea.
No sun, yet all around that inward light
Which is in purity,—a soft moonshine,
The silvery dimness of a happy dream.
How beautiful! afar on moorland ways,
Bosomed by mountains, darkened by huge glens,
(Where the lone altar raised by Druid hands
Stands like a mournful phantom), hidden clouds
Let fall soft beauty, till each green fir branch
Is plumed and tassel'd, till each heather stalk
Is delicately fringed. The sycamores,
Thro' all their mystical entanglement
Of boughs, are draped with silver. All the green
Of sweet leaves playing with the subtle air
In dainty murmuring; the obstinate drone
Of limber bees that in the monkshood bells
House diligent; the imperishable glow
Of summer sunshine never more confessed

The harmony of nature, the divine
Diffusive spirit of the Beautiful.
Out in the snowy dimness, half revealed
Like ghosts in glimpsing moonshine, wildly run
The children in bewildering delight.
There is a living glory in the air—
A glory in the hush'd air, in the soul
A palpitating wonder hush'd in awe.

Softly—with delicate softness—as the light
Quickens in the undawned east; and silently—
With definite silence—as the stealing dawn
Dapples the floating clouds, slow fall, slow fall,
With indecisive motion eddying down,
The white-winged flakes—calm as the sleep of sound,
Dim as a dream. The silver-misted air
Shines with mild radiance, as when thro' a cloud
Of semi-lucent vapour shines the moon.
I saw last evening (when the ruddy sun,

Enlarged and strange, sank low and visibly,
Spreading fierce orange o'er the west), a scene
Of winter in his milder mood. Green fields,
Which no kine cropped, lay damp; and naked trees
Threw skeleton shadows. Hedges thickly grown,
Twined into compact firmness with no leaves,
Trembled in jewelled fretwork as the sun
To lustre touched the tremulous waterdrops.
Alone, nor whistling as his fellows do
In fabling poem and provincial song,
The ploughboy shouted to his reeking team;
And at the clamour, from a neighbouring field
Arose, with whirr of wings, a flock of rooks
More clamorous; and thro' the frosted air,
Blown wildly here and there without a law,
They flew, low-grumbling out loquacious croaks.
Red sunset brightened all things; streams ran red
Yet coldly; and before the unwholesome east,
Searching the bones and breathing ice, blew down

The hill with a dry whistle, by the fire
In chamber twilight rested I at home.

But now what revelation of fair change,
O Giver of the seasons and the days !
Creator of all elements, pale mists,
Invisible great winds and exact frost !
How shall I speak the wonder of thy snow?
What though we know its essence and its birth,
Can quick expound in philosophic wise,
The how, and whence, and manner of its fall ;
Yet, oh, the inner beauty and the life—
The life that is in snow ! The virgin-soft
And utter purity of the down-flake
Falling upon its fellow with no sound !
Unblown by vulgar winds, innumerous flakes
Fall gently, with the gentleness of love !
Between its spotless-clothëd banks, in clear
Pellucid luculence, the Luggie seems

Charmed in its course, and with deceptive calm
Flows mazily in unapparent lapse,
A liquid silence. Every field is robed,
And in the furrow lies the plough unused.
The earth is cherished, for beneath the soft
Pure uniformity, is gently born
Warmth and rich mildness fitting the dead roots
For the resuscitation of the spring.

Now while I write, the wonder clothes the vale,
Calmed every wind and loaded every grove;
And looking thro' the implicated boughs
I see a gleaming radiance. Sparkling snow
Refined by morning-footed frost so still
Mantles each bough; and such a windless hush
Breathes thro' the air, it seems the fairy glen
About some phantom palace, pale abode
Of fabled *Sleeping Beauty*. Songless birds
Flit restlessly about the breathless wood,

Waiting the sudden breaking of the charm;
And as they quickly spring on nimble wing
From the white twig, a sparkling shower falls
Starlike. It is not whiteness, but a clear
Outshining of all purity, which takes
The winking eyes with such a silvery gleam.
No sunshine, and the sky is all one cloud.
The vale seems lonely, ghostlike; while aloud
The housewife's voice is heard with doubled sound.
I have not words to speak the perfect show;
The ravishment of beauty; the delight
Of silent purity; the sanctity
Of inspiration which o'erflows the world,
Making it breathless with divinity.
God makes His angels spirits—that is, winds—
His ministers a flaming fire. So, heart!
(Weak heart that fainted in thy loneliness)
In the sweet breezes spirits are alive;
God's angels guide the thunder-clouds; and God

Speaks in the thunder truly. All around
Is loving and continuous deity;
His mercy over all His works remains.
And surely in the glossy snow there shines
Angelic influence—a ministry
Devout and heavenly, that with benign
Action, amid a wondrous hush lets fall
The dazzling garment on the fostered fields.

So thus with fair delapsion softly falls
The sacred shower; and when the shortened day
Dejected dies in the low streaky west,
The rimy moon displays a cold blue night,
And keen as steel the east wind sprinkles ice.
Thicker than bees, about the waxing moon
Gather the punctual stars. Huge whitened hills
Rise glimmering to the blue verge of the night,
Ghostlike, and striped with narrow glens of firs
Black-waving, solemn. O'er the Luggie stream

Gathers a veiny film of ice, and creeps
With elfin feet around each stone and reed,
Working fine masonry; while o'er the dam
Dashing, a noise of waters fills the clear
And nitrous air. All the dark wintry hours
Sharply the winds from the white level moors
Keen whistle. Timorous in homely bed
The schoolboy listens, fearful lest gaunt wolves
Or beasts, whose uncouth forms in ancient books
He has beheld, at creaking shutters pull
Howling. And when at last the languid dawn
In windy redness re-illumes the east
With ineffectual fire, an intense blue
Severely vivid o'er the snowy hills
Gleams chill, while hazy half-transparent clouds
Slow-range the freezing ether of the west.
Along the woods the keenly vehement blasts
Wail, and disrobe the mantled boughs, and fling
A snow-dust everywhere. Thus wears the day:

While grandfather over the well-watched fire
Hangs cowering, with a cold drop at his nose.

Now underneath the ice the Luggie growls,
And to the polished smoothness curlers come
Rudely ambitious. Then for happy hours
The clinking stones are slid from wary hands,
And *Barleycorn*, best wine for surly airs,
Bites i' th' mouth, and ancient jokes are crack'd.
And oh, the journey homeward, when the sun,
Low-rounding to the west, in ruddy glow
Sinks large, and all the amber-skirted clouds,
His flaming retinue, with dark'ning glow
Diverge! The broom is brandished as the sign
Of conquest, and impetuously they boast
Of how this shot was played—with what a bend
Peculiar—the perfection of all art—
That stone came rolling grandly to the *Tee*
With victory crown'd, and flinging wide the rest

In lordly crash! Within the village inn,
What time the stars are sown in ether keen,
Clear and acute with brightness; and the moon
Sharpens her semicircle; and the air
With bleakly shivering sough cuts like a scythe,
They by the roaring chimney sit, and quaff
The beaded '*Usqueba*' with sugar dash'd.
Oh, when the precious liquid fires the brain
To joy, and every heart beats fast with mirth
And ancient fellowship, what nervy grasps
Of horny hands o'er tables of rough oak!
What singing of *Lang Syne* till teardrops shine
And friendships brighten as the evening wanes!

Now the dead earth, wrapt solemnly, expects
The punctual resurrection of the Spring.
Shackled and bound, the coldly vigilant frost
Stiffens all rivers, and with eager power
Hardens each glebe. The wasted country owns

The keen despotic vehemence of the North;
And, with the resignation that obtains
Where he is weak and powerless, man awaits,
Under God's mercy, the dissolvent thaw.

O All-beholding, All-informing God
Invisible, and ONLY through effects
Known and belov'd, unshackle the waste earth!
Soul of the incomplete vitality
In atom and in man! Soul of all Worlds!
Leave not Thy glory vacant, nor afflict
With fear and hunger man whom Thou hast made.
Thou from Thy chambers waterest the earth;
Thou givest snow like wool; and scatterest wide
Hoarfrost like ashes. Casting forth Thy ice
Like morsels, who can stand before Thy cold?
Thou sendest forth Thy word, and lo! they melt;
Causing Thy wind to blow, the waters flow.*

* Psalm cxlvii. 16-18.

Soon the frozen air receives the subtle thaw :
And suddenly a crawling mist, with rain
Impregn'd, the damp day dims, and drizzling drops
Proclaim a change. At night across the heavens
Swift-journeying, and by a furious wind
Squadron'd, the hurrying clouds range the roused sky,
Magnificently sombrous. The wan moon,
Amazed, gleams often through a cloudy rack,
Then, shuddering, hides. One earnest wakeful star
Of living sapphire drooping by her side,
A faithful spirit in her lone despair,
Outshines the cloudy tempest. Then the shower
Falls ceaseless, and night murmurs with the rain.
And in the sounding morning what a change !
The meadows shine new-washed; while here and there
A dusky patch of snow in shelter'd paths
Melts lonely. The awakened forest waves
With boughs unplumed. The white investiture

Of the fair earth hath vanished, and the hills
That in the evening sunset glowed with rose
And ineffectual baptism of gold,
Shine tawdry, crawled upon by the blind rain.
Now Luggie thunders down the ringing vale,
Tawnily brown, wide-leaving yellow sand
Upon the meadow. The South-West, aroused,
Blustering in moody kindness, clears the sky
To its blue depths by a full-wingëd wind,
Blowing the diapason of red March.

Blow high and cleanse the sky, O South-West wind !
Roll the full clouds obedient; overthrow
White crags of vapour in confusion piled
Precipitate, high-toppling, undissolved ;
And while with silent workings they are spread
And scattered, broken into ruinous pomp
By Thy invisible influence, what calm
And sweet disclosure of the upper deep

Cerulean, the atmospheric sea!
Blow high and sift the earth, thou South-West wind!
Now the dull air grows rarer, and no more
The stark day thickens towards evenfall;
Nor from the solid cloud-gloom drips the rain:
But in a sunset mild and beautiful
The day sinks, till in clear dilucid air,
As in a chamber newly decorate,
The golden Phœbe reddens with the wind.
No more through hoary mists and low-hung clouds
The eternal hills—bones of the earth—upheave
Their deity for worship: but severe
Against the clear sky outlined, each sharp crag
Uplifts its scarred magnificence to Heaven.
From breezy ledge the eagle springs aloft,
And, beating boldly up against the wind
With inconceivable velocity,
Stretches to upper ether, and renews
Haughty communion with the regal sun!

Blow high, O deep-mouth'd wind from the South-
  West!
And in the caves and hollows of the rocks
Moan mournfully, for desolation reigns.
Through the unknown abysses and foul chasms,
Sacred to horror and eternal damps
And darkness ever-cumbent, blindly howl
Till the hoarse dragons, wailing in their woe
Infernal, answer from accursed dens.

Pleasant to him who long in sick-room pent,
Surveying still the same unchanging hills
Belted with vapour, muffled up in cloud;
The same raw landscape soaked in ceaseless rain;
Pleasant to him the invigorating wind.
Roused from reclusive thought by the deep sound
And motion of the forest (as a steed
When shrills the silver trumpet of the onset),
He rushes to communion with old forms.

Like a fair picture suddenly uncovered
To an impatient artist, the fair earth,
Touched with the primal glory of the Spring,
Flings an indefinite glamour on his soul.
With indistinct commotion he perceives
All things, and his delight is indistinct.
Earth's forms and ever-living beauty strike
Amazement through his spirit, till he feels
As one new-born to being undeflowered.
The sudden music from the budding woods,
The lark in air, startles and overjoys.
O Laverock! (for thy Scottish name to me
Sounds sweetest) with unutterable love
I love thee, for each morning as I lie
Relaxed and weary with my long disease,
One from low grass arises visibly
And sings as if it sang for me alone.
Among a thousand I could tell the tones
Of this, my little sweet hierophant!

To fainting heart and the despairing soul
What is more soothing than the natural voice
Of birds? One Candlemas, many years ago,
When weak with pain and sickness, it infused
Into my soul a bliss delectable.
For suddenly into the misty air
A mellow, smooth and liquid music, clear
As silver, softer than an organ stop
Ere the bass grumbles, rose. The blunted winds,
No longer edged severely with keen frost,
Forgot to whisper, and a summer-calm
Pervaded soul and sense. No violet
As yet breathed perfume; from the darkling sward
No snowdrop boldly peeped; and even the ash,
Whence flowed the sound, unfolded not her buds
To blacken while the embryo gathered green.
And yet this hardy herald of the Spring
Chaunted rich harmony, daintily carved out
Her voice, and through her sleek throat sobb'd her
    soul

In a delicious tremble. As she tuned
Her pliant song, slow from the closing sky
The sacred snow fell calm. Yet through the shower,
Hushing all nature into silence, clear
The *Feltie-flier** trilled her slippery close
In panting rapture, from the whitening ash.
I stood all wonder; and to this late hour
Remember the dear song with ravishment;
Nor ever comes a merry Candlemas day
But I am out to hear. And if perchance
Some warbler sprinkle on the vacant air
Its homeless notes, the bird seems to my heart
The individual bird of comely grey
That sang her pliant strain through falling snow.

Now, when the crumbling glebe is by the wind
Unbound, and snows adown the mountains hoar

---

* I am almost certain this name of the bird is merely local, but I know no other.—[Mr. Robt. Gray, a well-known authority, says the bird alluded to is the Missel-Thrush.—ED.]

Glide liquid, from the furrow loose the plough.
Enyoke the willing horses, and upturn
With deep-pressed share the saponaceous loam.
From morn to even with progression slow
The ploughboy cuts his awkward parallels,
And soberly imbrowns the decent fields.
It was a hazy February day
Ten years ago, when I, a boy of ten,
Beheld a country ploughing-match. The morn
Lighted the east with a dim smoky flare
Of leaden purple, as the rumbling wains
Each with a plough light-laden (while behind
Trotted a horse sleek-comb'd and tail bedight
With many coloured ribbons) by our home
Went downwards to the rich fat meadow-grounds
Bounding the Luggie. Many a herd of beeves
Dew-lapp'd had fattened there, and headlong oft
O'er the hoof-clattering turf they wildly ran,
Lashing with swinging tail the thirsty flies.

But now the smooth expanse of level green
Was quickly to be changed to sober brown;
And twenty ploughs by twenty ploughmen held
To cut with shining share the living turf.
Oh many a wintry hour, thro' wind and rain,
In valleys gloom'd, or by the bleak hill-side
Lonely, these twenty had themselves inured
And stubborn'd to perfection. Many a touch
And word of honest kindness had been used
To the dear faithful horses *snooving* on
In quiet patience, jutting noble chests.
Now the big day, expected long, was come:
And, with proud shoulders yoked, conscious they
    stood
Patient and unrefusing; while behind,
All ready stripped, brown brawny arms displayed—
Arms sinewed by long labour—eager swains
O'er-leaning slight, with cautious wary hold
The plough detain. At the commencing sign

A simultaneous noise discordant tears
The air thick-closing to a hazy damp.
Sudden the horses move, and the clear yokes,
Well polished, clatter. With an artful bend
The gleaming coulter takes the grass and cuts
The greenly tedded blades with nibbling noise
Almost unheard. The smooth share follows fast;
And from its shining slope the clayey glebe
In neat and neighbouring furrows sidelong falls.
Thus till the dank, raw-cold, and unpurged day
Gathering its rheumy humours threatens rain;
And the bleak night steals up the forlorn east.
And when the careful verdict is preferr'd
By the wise judge (a gray-hair'd husbandman,
Himself in his fresh youth a ploughboy keen),
Some bosoms fire exultant. Others, slow
Their reeking horses harnessed, lag along
Heart-sad and weary; and the rumbling noise
Of homeward-going carts for miles away

Is heard, till night brings silence and repose.

But never with sad motions of the soul,
Despairing, yoked his sleek and smoking team
For homeward journey my belovëd friend!
He the great prize, the guinea all of gold,
Gained thrice and grew a very famous man;
Till Death, the churl accurs'd, him in his prime
Bore to the border-land of wonder. Then
I felt the blank in life when dies a friend.
Inexplicable emptiness and want
Unsatisfied! The unrepealable law
Consumed the living while the dead decayed.
No more, no more thro' glorious nights of May
We wander, chasing pleasure as of old.
First night of May! and the soft-silvered moon
Brightens her semi-circle in the blue;
And 'mid the tawny orange of the west
Shines the full star that ushers in the even!

On the low meadows by the Luggie-side
Gathers a semi-lucent mist, and creeps
In busy silence, shrouding golden furze
And leafy copsewood. Thro' the tortuous dell
Like an eternal sound the Luggie flows
In unreposing melody. And here,
Three perfect summers gone, my dear first friend
Was with me; and we swore a sudden oath,
To travel half-a-dozen miles and court
Two sisters, whose sweet faces sunshine kissed
To berry brown and country comeliness—
Kiss-worthier than the love of Solomon.
So singing clearly with a merry heart
Old songs—*It was upon a Lammas nicht;*
And that sweet thing by gentle Tannahill,
Married to music sweeter than itself,
The Lowland Lassie—thro' dew-silvered fields
We hastened 'mid the mist our footsteps raised
Until we reached the moorland. From its bed

Among the purplish heather whirring rose
The plover, wildly screaming; and from glens
Of moaning firs the pheasant's piercing shriek
Discordant sounded. Then, 'mong elder trees
Throwing antique fat shadows, soon we saw
The window panes, moon-whitened; and low heard
Bawtie, the shaggie collie, grumble out
His disapproval in a sullen growl.
But slyly wearing nearer, cried my friend,
"Whisht, Bawtie! Bawtie!" and the fellow came
Whining, and laid a wet nose in his palm
Obedient, while I tinkled on the panes
A fairy summons to the souls within.
The door creaked musically, and a face
Peeped smiling, till I whispered, "Open, Kate!"
And thro' the moonshine came the low sweet quest—
"Oh! is it you?" My answer was a kiss.
Then entering the kitchen paved with stone,
We kicked the sparkling faggot till it blazed;

And sitting round it, many a tale of love
Was told, until the chrysolite of dawn
Burned in the east, and from the mountain rolled
The sarcenet mists far-flaming with the morn.
This was my first of May three years ago:
Now in a churchyard by the Bothlin side—
The Auld Aisle—moulders my first friend, and keeps
An early tryste with God, the All in All.

We sat at school together on one seat,
Came home together thro' the lanes, and knew
The dunnock's nest together in the hedge,
With smooth blue eggs in cosy brightness warm.
And as two youngling kine on cold Spring nights
Lie close together on the bleak hill-side
For mutual heat, so when a trouble came
We crept to one another, growing still
True friends in interchange of heart and soul.
But suddenly death changed his countenance,

And grav'd him in the darkness far from me.
O Friendship, prelibation of divine
Enjoyment, union exquisite of soul,
How many blessings do I owe to thee,
How much of incommunicable woe!
The daisies bloom among the tall green blades
Upon his grave, and listening you may hear
The Bothlin make sweet music as she flows;
And you may see the poplars by her brink
Twinkle their silvery leaflets in the sun.
O little wandering preacher, Bothlin brook!
Wind musically by his lonely grave.
O well-known face, for ever lost! and voice,
For ever silent! I have heard thee sing
In village inns what time the silver frost
Curtained the panes in silent ministry,
Sing old Scotch ballads full of love and woe,
While the assimilative snow fell white and calm
With ceaseless lapse. And I have seen thee dance

c

Wild galliards with the buxom lasses, far
In lone farm-houses set on whistling hills,
While the storm thickened into thunder-cloud.
Dear mentor in all rustic merriment,
Ever as hearty as the night was long!
I miss thee often, as I do to-night,
And my heart fills; and thy belovëd songs
The music and the words ring in my ears,
Then Lowland lassie wilt thou go—until
My eyes are full of tears, dear heart! dear heart!
And I could pass the perilous edge of death
To see thy dear, dear face, and hear again
The old wild music as of old, of old.

But as the Luggie with a plaintive song
'Twists thro' a glen of greenest gloom, and gropes
For open sunshine; and, the shadows past,
Glides quicker-footed thro' divided meads
With sliding purl, so from that tale of gloom

My song with happier motions seeks the calm
And quiet smoothness of a silver end.
From orient valleys where as lucent dew
As ever jewelled Hermon, falls and shines
Fulfilled by sunrise; where slant arrow-showers
Of golden beams make every twinkling drop
A diamond, and every blade of grass
A glory;—comes the earth-born wanderer
Sweet Luggie, singing. Over the mill-dam
Sounding, a cataract in miniature,
White-robed it dashes thro' unceasing mist.
Thro' ivied bridge, adown its rocky bed
Shadowed by wavy limes whose branches bend
Kissing the wave to ripples, on it purls
Abrupt, capricious, past the hazel bower
Where marriageable maid is being woo'd;
And as on sward of velvet by her side
Her lover low reclines, while his dear tongue
Voices warm passion—she confiding lays

All her mild beauty in his manly breast
Blushing. Ah, Luggie! sure you murmur now
Clearly and dearly o'er thy pumy stones!
And when amid a pause of thought they hear
Thy babblement of music, never a shade
Darkens their souls. Thy song is happiness,
A revelation of sweet sympathies
By them interpreted; for never yet
Was Nature sullen when the spirit shone.
This is in twilight, when that only star
White Hesperus from chastest azure grows;
And as night trails her thousand shadows slow
Over the spinning world, the streamlet sings
Her mother earth asleep. O Autumn nights!
When skies are deeply blue, and the full moon
Soars in voluptuous whiteness, Juno-like,
A passionate splendour; when in the great south
Orion like a frozen skeleton
Hints of his ancient hugeness and mail'd strength;

And Cassiopeia glimmers cold and clear
Upon her throne of seven diamonds!
In the thick-foliaged brake, the nightingale
Of Scotland, chirping stonechacker, prolongs
With *whit, whit, chirr-r* the day's full melody.
Far-sounding thro' blue silence and smooth air,
The drumming noise of the hoarse waterfall
Is heard unheeded all by homely fires,
And heard unheeded all in hazel bower
Where love wings hours of serene joy; and still
As roams with *eerie* wail the unbodied wind
Thro' ghostly glen of pine, the maiden clings
More closely, till two firm entwining arms
Press comfort; and there is a touch of lips.

Now in this season—ere the flickering leaves,
Touch'd with October's fiery alchemy,
Grow sere and crisp—is shorn the meadow-hay.
Mingled with spiral orchis, dim blue-bell

Of delicatest azure, crowfoot smooth,
And ox-eye flaunting with faint flowers wild,
Nameless to me—the fragrant rye-grass grew.
Now with a measured sweep the keen-edged scythe
Cuts all to wither in the imbrowning sun.
Two golden days o'erpast (with eves of cloud
Magnificently coloured, heaped and strewn
Confusedly) the country lasses come
Bare-armed, bare-ancled; and 'mid honest mirth
And homely jests with tinkling laughter winged,
Gather the fading balm. With kindling eyes,
And all the life of maidenhood aflame
In little tremulous pants,—they carry light
The warm load to the stack.

                              Oh, many a time
The old man, building slow the rising stack,
Saw and reproved not our wild merriment:
Remembering, half-sad, his own fresh youth
When beauty was a magic to the soul

And a fair face a charm; when a lip-touch
Was necromancy; and the perfect life
A wondrous yearning after womanhood.
But at the breathless nerve-dissolving noon,
When hot the undiminished sun downthrows
Direct his beams, they from the field retire
To cool consoling grove, or haply seek
The drowsy pool by beechen shadow chilled,
To lave the limbs relaxed. With eager leap,
Headlong they plunge from the enamelled bank
Into the liquid cold, and slowly move
With measured strokes and palms outspread; while oft,
When the clear water rises o'er the lip
Dallying, they uptilt the swelling chest
In unspent vigour.

      Oh, the pleasant time!
Pleasant beneath embowering trees, when day
Hides with her silken mists the distant scene
And breathes afar a nerve-dissolving steam—

Pleasant in sweet consolatory shade
To wander pensive. Then the soul serenes
The turbulent passions, and in devout trance,
Unconscious of celestial power, reveals
The God reflected in fair natural forms.
For as the Sun disdains the vulgar gaze
In his uplifted sphere, yet in the broad
Grey Ocean shews a softer face, so God
In nature shines. Oh, sweet the bowery path
Of fair Glenconner, where in volant youth
I saw the heroes of divine Romance.
No pathway winding through fresh orange groves,
Leading to white Campanian city, set
Inviolably by the sapphire sea,
Can fair Glenconner's umbrage-shadowed way
Excel. The bird-embowering beechen boughs,
Kissing each other, on the dusty way
Throw trembling shadows; and when warm west
    winds

Roam hither in voluptuous unconcern,

There is a music and a fragrancy

Upon Glenconner, like the music hymned

By quires angelic on cerulean floors.

Deem not I speak in vanity, or speak

In false hyperbole, as poets do

When languaging in love the radiance

Of maids; but there is beauty and delight

And passive feeling sweeter than all sense,

To him who walks beneath the boughs, and hears

The humming music like the sound of seas.

There have I dreamed for hours—and gathered there

The homely inspiration which fulfils

The yearning of my soul. There have I felt

The unconfined divinity which lies

In beauty; and when the eternal stars

Have twinkled silver thro' illumined leaves,

I could not choose but worship.

O fair eves
Of undescribable sweetness long ago!
When gloaming caught me musing unawares,
Musing alone beneath the whispering leaves
That overshade Glenconner. Hour of calm
Suggestive thought, when, like a robe, the earth
Puts on a shadowy pensiveness, and stills
The music of her motions multiform.
Day lingered in the west; and thro' a sky
Of thinly-waning orange, sullen clouds
Of amethyst, with flamy purple edged,
Moved evenly in sluggish pilotage.
The windless shades of quiet eventide
Slow gathered, and the sweet concordant tones
Of melody within the leafy brake
Died clearly, till the Mavis piped alone;
Then softly from the jasper sky, a star
Drew radiant silver, brightening as the west
Darkened. But ere the semicircled moon

Shed her white light adown the lucent air,

The Mavis ceased, and thro' the thin gloom brake

The Corncraik's curious cry, the sylvan voice

Of the shy bird that haunts the bladed corn;

And suddenly, yet silently, the blue

Deepened, until innumerous white stars

Thro' crystal smooth and yielding ether drooped,

Not coldly, but in passionate June glow.

The Corncraik now, 'mong tall green bladed corn

Breasted her eggs with feathers dew-besprent,

And stayed her human cry. The silence left

A gap within the soul, a sudden grief,

An emptiness in the low sighing air.

Then swooning through full night, the summer'd earth

Bosom'd her children into tender rest;

Now delicately chambered ladies breathe

Their souls asleep in white-limb'd luxury.

O Virgins purest lipped! with snowy lids

Soft closed on living eyes! O unkissed cheeks,
Half-sunk in pillowy pressure, and round arms
In the sweet pettishness of silver dreams
Flung warm into the cold unheeding air!
Sleep! soft bedewer of infantine eyes,
Pouter of rosy little lips! plump hands
Are doubled into deeply-dimpled fists
And stretched in rosy langour, curls are laid
In fragrance on the rounded baby-face,
Kiss-worthy darling! Stiller of clear tongues
And silvery laughter! Now the musical noise
Of little feet is silent, and blue shoes
No more come pattering from the nursery door.
Death is not of thee, Sleep! Thy calm domain
Is tempered with a dreamy bliss, and dimmed
With haunted glooms, and richly sanctified
With the fine elements of Paradise.
Burn in the gleaming sky, ye far-off Stars!
And thou, O inoffensive Crescent! lift

The wonder of thy softness, the white shell
Of thy clear beauty, till the wholesome dawn
Wither thy brightness pale, and borrowed pride!

But sleep supine, on indolent afternoon
Ere the winds wake, and holy mountain airs
Descend, is sweet. Oh, let the bard describe
The sacred spot where, underneath the round
Green odoriferous sycamore, he lay
Sleepless, yet half-asleep, in that one mood
When the quick sense is duped, and angel wings
Make spiritual music. Sweet and dim
The sacred spot, belovëd not alone
For its own beauty: but the memories,
The pictures of the past which in the mind
Arise in fair profusion, each distinct
With the soft hue of some peculiar mood,
Enchant to living lustre what before
Was to the untaught vision simply fair.

In a fair valley, carpeted with turf
Elastic, sloping upwards from the stream,
A rounded sycamore in honied leaves
Most plenteous, murmurous with humming bees,
Shadows a well. Darkly the crystal wave
Gleams cold, secluded; on its polished breast
Imaging twining boughs. No pitcher breaks
Its natural sleep, except at morn and eve
When my good mother thro' the dewy grass
Walks patient with her vessels, bringing home
The clear refreshment. Every blowing Spring,
A snowdrop, with pure streaks of delicate green
Upon its inmost leaves, from withered grass
Springs whitely, and within its limpid breast
Is mirror'd whitely. Not a finger plucks
This hidden beauty; but it blooms and dies,
In lonely lustre blooms and lonely dies—
Unknown, unloved, save by one simple heart
Poetic, the creator of this song.

And after this frail luxury hath given
Its little life in keeping to the soul
Of all the worlds, a robin builds its nest
In lowly cleft, a foot or so above
The water. His dried leaves, and moss, and grass
He hither carries, lining all with hair
For softness. I have laid the hand that writes
These rhymes belovëd, on the crimson breast,
Sleek-soft, that panted o'er the five unborn;
While, leaf-hid, o'er me sang the watchful mate
Plaintive, and with a sorrow in the song,
In silvan nook where anchoret might dwell
Contented. Often on September days,
When woods were efflorescent, and the fields
Refulgent with the bounty of the corn,
And warming sunshine filled the breathless air
With a pale steam,—in heart-confused mood
Have I worn holidays enraptured there;
For, O dear God! there is a pure delight

In dreaming: in those mental-weary times,
When the vext spirit finds a false content
In fashioning delusions. Oh, to lie
Supinely stretched upon the shaded turf,
Beholding thro' the openings of green leaves
White clouds in silence navigating slow
Cerulean seas illimitable! Hushed
The drowsy noon, and, with a stilly sound
Like harmony of thought, the Luggie frets—
Its bubbling mellowed to a musical hum
By distance. Then the influences faint,
Those visionary impulses that swell
The soul to inspiration, crowding come
Mysterious: and phantom memory
(Ghost of dead feeling) haunts the undissolved,
The unsubvertive temple of the soul!

But as thro' loamy meadows lipping slow
Eats the fern-fringëd Luggie; and in spray

Leaps the mill-dam, and o'er the rocky flats
Spreads in black eddies; so my firstborn song
Hastes to the end in heedless vagrancy.
O ravishingly sweet the clacking noise
Of looms that murmur in our quiet dell!
No fairer valley Dyer ever dreamed—
Dyer, best river-singer, bard among
Ten thousand. Reader, hasten ye and come,
And see the Luggie wind her liquid stream
Thro' copsy villages and spiry towns;
And see the Bothlin trotting swift of foot
From glades of alder, eager to combine
Her dimpling harmony with Luggie's calm
Clear music, like the music of the soul.
But where you see the meeting, reader, stay,
O stay and hear the music of the looms.
Thro' homely rustic bridge with ivy shagged
(Which you shall see if ever you do come
A summer pilgrim to our valley fair),

The Luggie flows with bells of foam-like stars
About its surface. A smooth bleaching-green
Spreads its soft carpet to the open doors
Of simple houses, shining-white. Blue smoke
Curls thro' the breathing air to the tree-tops
Thin spreading, and is lost. A humming noise
Industrious is heard, the clack of looms,
Whereon sit maidens, homely fair, and full
Of household simpleness, who sing and weave,
And sing and weave thro' all the easy hours,
Each day to-morrow's counterpart, and smooth
Memory the mirror wherein golden Hope,
Contented, sees herself. Here dwell an old
Couple whose lives have known twice forty years
(My mother's parents), their sage spirits touched
With blest anticipation of a home
Celestial bright, wherein they may fulfil
The life which death discovers. Last winter night
I, an accustomed visitant, beheld

The dear old pair. He in an easy chair
Lay dozing, while beside her noiseless wheel
She sat, her brow into her lap declined,
And half asleep! Sure sign, my mother said,
Of the conclusion of mortality.
A boy of ten, their grandson, on the floor
Lay stretched in early slumber; all the three
Unconscious of my entrance. A strange sight,
Fraught with strange lessons for the human soul.
In the first portion of her married life,
This woman, now, alas! so weary, old,
Bore daughters five; of well-beloved sons
An equal number. Some of them died young,
But six are yet alive, and dwelling all
Within a mile of her own house. The flower,
The idol of the mother, and her pride,
Dear magnet of all hopes, embodiment
Of heavenly blessings, was the youngest son,
Youngest of all. Me often has she told

How not a man could fling the stone with him;
That in his shoes he outran racers fleet
Barefooted; dancing on the shaven green
On summer holidays and autumn eves
(As to this day they do) his laugh was clearest,
Lightest his step; and he could thrill the hearts
Of simple women by a natural grace,
And perilous recital of love tales.
I cannot tell by what mysterious means,
Day-dream, or silver vision of the night,
Or sacred show of reason, picturing
A smooth ambition and calm happiness
For years of weaker age—but suddenly
In prime of life there flowered in his soul
An inextinguishable love to be
A minister of God. When holy schemes
Govern the motions of the spirit, ways
Are found to compass them. With wary care,
Frugality praiseworthy, and the strength

Of two strong arms, he in the summer months
Hoarded a competence equivalent
To all demands, until the session's end.
Whate'er by manual labour he had gained
Thro' the clear summer months in verdant fields,
With brooks of silver laced, and cool'd with winds,
Was spent in winter in the smoky town.
But when, his annual course of study past,
He with his presence blessed his father's house,
With what a sacred sanctity of hope
Eager his mother dreamed, or garrulous
Spake of him everywhere—his foreign ways,
And midnight porings o'er *uncanny* books.
His father, with a stern delight suffused,
Grew a proud man of some importance now
In his own eyes; for who in all the vale
Had e'er a son so noble and so learned,
So worthy as his own?
So time wore on: but when three years complete

Had perfected their separate destinies,
A change stole o'er the current of their lives,
As a cloud-shadow glooms the crystal stream.
Their son came home, but with his coming came
Sorrow. A hue too beautifully fair
Brighten'd his cheek, as sunlight tints a cloud.
His face had caught a trick of joy more sad
Than visible grief; and all the subtle frame
Of human life, so wonderfully wrought,
A mystery of mechanism, was wearing
In sore uneasy manner to the grave.
What need to tell what every heart must know
In sympathy prophetical? Long time,
A varied year in seasons four complete
(For the white snow-drop o'er my mother's well
Twice oped its whitest leaves among the green),
He lay consuming. It must needs have been
A weary trial to the thinking soul,
Thus with a consciousness of coming death,

The grim Attenuation! evermore
Nearing insatiate. At her spinning-wheel
His mother sat; and when his voice grew faint,
A simple whistle by his pillow lay,
And at its sound she entered patient, sad,
Her soothing love to minister, her hope
To nourish to its fading. But his breath
Grew weaker ever; and his dry pale lips
Closing upon the little instrument,
Could not produce a faintly audible note!
A little bell, the plaything of a child,
Now at his bedside hung, and its clear tones
Tinkled the weary summons. Thus his time
Narrowed to a completion, and his soul,
Immortal in its nature, thro' his eyes
Yearning, beheld the majesty of Him
Great in His mystery of godliness,
Fulfiller of the dim Apocalypse!

Twelve years have passed since then, and he is now
A happy memory in the hearts of those
Who knew him; for to know him was to love.
And oft I deem it better, as the fates,
Or God, whose will is fate, have proven it;
For had he lived and fallen (as who of us
Doth perfectly? and let him that is proud
Take heed lest he do fall) he would have been
A sadness to them in their aged hours.
But now he is an honour and delight;
A treasure of the memory; a joy
Unutterable: by the lone fireside
They never tire to speak his praise, and say
How, if he had been spared, he would have been
So great, and good, and noble as (they say)
The country knows; although I know full well
That not a man in all the parish round
Speaks of him ever; he is now forgot,
And this his natal valley knows him not.—

And this his natal valley knows him not?
The well-belovëd, nothing?—the fair face
And pliant limbs, poor indistinctive dust?
The body, blood, and network of the brain
Crumbled as a clod crumbles! Is this all?
A turf, a date, an epitaph, and then
Oblivion, and profound nonentity!
And thus his natal valley knows him not.
Trees murmur to the passing wind, streams flow,
Flowers shine with dewdrops in the shady glens,
All unintelligent creation smiles
In loving-kindness; but, like a light dream
Of morning, man arises in fair show,
Like the hued rainbow from incumbent gloom
Elicited, he shines against the sun—
A momentary glory. Not a voice
Remains to whisper of his whereabouts:
The palpable body in its mother's breast
Dissolves, and every feature of the face

Is lost in feculent changes. O black earth!
Wrap from bare eyes the slow decaying form,
The beauty rotting from the living hair,
The body made incapable thro' sin
God's Spirit to contain. Earth, wrap it close
Till the heavens vibrate to the trump of doom!

This is not all: for the invisible soul
Betrays the soft desire, the quenchless wish,
To live a purer life, more proximate
To the prime Fountain of all life. The power
Of vivid fancy and the boundless scenes
(High coloured with the colouring of Heaven),
Creations of imagination, tell
The mortal yearnings of immortal souls!
Now, while around me in blind labour winds
Howl, and the rain-drops lash the streaming pane;
Now, while the pine-glen on the mountain side
Roars in its wrestling with the sightless foe,

And the black tarn grows hoary with the storm ;—
Amid the external elemental war,
My soul with calm comportment—more becalmed
By the wild tempest furious without—
Sits in her sacred cell, and ruminates
On Death, severe discloser of new life.
When the well-known and once embraceable form
Is but a handful of white dust, the soul
Grows in divine dilation, nearer God.
Therefore grieve not, my heart, that unsustained
His memory died among us, that no more,
While yet the grass is hoary and the dawn
Lingers, he shyly thro' untrodden fields
Brushes his early path : that he no more
Beneath the beech, in lassitude outstretched,
Ponders the holy strains of Israel's King;
For in translated glory, and new clothed
With Incorruptible, he purer air
Breathes in a fairer valley. There no storm

Maddens as now; no flux, and no opaque,
But all is calm, and permanent, and clear,
God's glory and the Lamb illumine all!

Now ends this song—not for self-honour sung,
But in the Luggie's service. It hath been
A crownëd vision and a silver dream,
That I should touch this valley with renown
Eternal, make the fretting waters gleam
In light above the common light of earth.
The shoreless air of heaven is purer here,
The golden beams more keenly crystalline,
The skies more deeply sapphired. For to me,
About these emerald fields and lawny hills,
There linger glories which you cannot see,
And influences which you cannot feel,
Delight and incommunicable woe!
My home is here; and like a patient star,
Shining between untroubled Paradise

And my own soul, a mother shines therein,
The sole perfection of true womanhood :
A father—with the wisdom which pertains
To grey experience, and that stern delight
In naked truth, and reason which belongs
To the intense reflective mind—hath told
His fifty winters here. And all the hopes
Which gild the present; all the sad regrets
Which dull the past, are present to my soul
In the external forms and colourings
Of this dear valley. Therefore do I yearn
To make its stream flow in undying verse,
Low-singing thro' the labyrinthine dell!

And let forgiving charity preclude
Harsh judgments from the singer: not that he
Fearfully would forestal the righteous word,
Blameworthy, spoken in kindness, and that truth
Which sanctions condemnation. Yet, dear Lord,

A youthful flattering of the spirit, touched
With a desire unquenchable, displays
My hope's delirium. Oh! if the dream
Fade into nothing, into worse than nought,
Blackness of darkness like the golden zones
Of an autumnal sunset, and the night
Of unfulfilled ambition closes round
My destiny, think what an awful hell
O'erwhelms the conquer'd soul! Therefore, O men
Who guard with jealousy and loving care
The honour of our sacred literature,
Read with a kindness born of trustful hope,
Forgiving rambling schoolboy thoughts, too plain
To utter with a spasm, or clothe in cold
Mosaic fretwork of well-pleasing words,
Forgiving youth's vagaries, want of skill,
And blind devotional passion for my home!

In the Shadows.

A POEM IN SONNETS.

Induction.

ENTER, scared mortal! and in awe behold
　　The chancel of a dying poet's mind,
Hung round, ah! not adorned, with pictures bold
And quaint, but roughly touched for the refined.
The chancel not the charnel house! For I
To God have raised a shrine immaculate
Therein, whereon His name to glorify,
And daily mercies meekly celebrate.
So in, scared breather! here no hint of death—
Skull or cross-bones suggesting sceptic fear;
Yea rather calmer beauty, purer breath
Inhaled from a diviner atmosphere.

I.

IF it must be; if it must be, O God!
    That I die young, and make no further moans;
That, underneath the unrespective sod,
    In unescutcheoned privacy, my bones
Shall crumble soon,—then give me strength to bear
    The last convulsive throe of too sweet breath!
I tremble from the edge of life, to dare
    The dark and fatal leap, having no faith,
No glorious yearning for the Apocalypse;
    But, like a child that in the night-time cries
For light, I cry; forgetting the eclipse
    Of knowledge and our human destinies.
O peevish and uncertain soul! obey
The law of life in patience till the Day.

II.

"WHOM the gods love die young." The thought
    is old;
And yet it soothed the sweet Athenian mind.
I take it with all pleasure, overbold,
    Perhaps, yet to its virtue much inclined
By an inherent love for what is fair.
    This is the utter poetry of woe—
That the bright-flashing gods should cure despair
    By love, and make youth precious here below.
I die, being young; and, dying, could become
    A pagan, with the tender Grecian trust.
Let death, the fell anatomy, benumb
    The hand that writes, and fill my mouth with
        dust—
Chant no funereal theme, but, with a choral
Hymn, O ye mourners! hail immortal youth au-
    roral!

III.

WITH the tear-worthy four, consumption killed
    In youthfnl prime, before the nebulous mind
Had its symmetric shapeliness defined,
Had its transcendent destiny fulfilled.—
  May future ages grant me gracious room,
With Pollok, in the voiceless solitude
  Finding his holiest rapture, happiest mood;
Poor White for ever poring o'er the tomb;
  With Keats, whose lucid fancy mounting far
Saw heaven as an intenser, a more keen
Redintegration of the Beauty seen
    And felt by all the breathers on this star;
With gentle Bruce, flinging melodious blame
Upon the Fnture for an uncompleted name.'

IV.

OH many a time with Ovid have I borne
   My father's vain, yet well-meant reprimand,
To leave the sweet-air'd, clover-purpled land
Of rhyme—its Lares loftily forlorn,
With all their pure humanities unworn—
   To batten on the bare Theologies!
   To quench a glory lighted at the skies,
Fed on one essence with the silver morn,
   Were of all blasphemies the most insane.
So deeplier given to the delicious spell
   I clung to thee, heart-soothing Poesy!
Now on a sick-bed rack'd with arrowy pain
   I lift white hands of gratitude, and cry,
Spirit of God in Milton! was it well?

V.

Last night, on coughing slightly with sharp pain,
    There came arterial blood, and with a sigh
Of absolute grief I cried in bitter vein,
    That drop is my death-warrant: I must die.
Poor meagre life is mine, meagre and poor!
    Rather a piece of childhood thrown away;
An adumbration faint; the overture
    To stifled music; year that ends in May;
The sweet beginning of a tale unknown;
    A dream unspoken; promise unfulfilled;
A morning with no noon, a rose unblown—
    All its deep rich vermilion crushed and killed
I' th' bud by frost:—Thus in false fear I cried,
Forgetting that to abolish death Christ died.

VI.

SWEETLY, my mother! Go not yet away—
    I have not told my story. Oh, not yet,
With the fair past before me, can I lay
    My cheek upon the pillow to forget.
O sweet, fair past, my twenty years of youth
    Thus thrown away, not fashioning a man;
But fashioning a memory, forsooth!
    More feminine than follower of Pan.
O God! let me not die for years and more!
    Fulfil Thyself, and I will live then surely
Longer than a mere childhood. Now heart-sore,
    Weary, with being weary—weary, purely.
In dying, mother, I can find no pleasure
Except in being near thee without measure.

VII.

Hew Atlas for my monument; upraise
    A pyramid for my tomb, that, undestroyed
    By rank, oblivion, and the hungry void,
My name shall echo through prospective days.
    O careless conqueror! cold, abysmal grave!
Is it not sad—is it not sad, my heart—
To smother young ambition, and depart
    Unhonoured and unwilling, like death's slave?
No rare immortal remnant of my thought
    Embalms my life; no poem, firmly reared
    Against the shock of time, ignobly feared—
But all my life's progression come to nought.
    Hew Atlas! build a pyramid in a plain!
    Oh, cool the fever burning in my brain!

VIII.

FROM this entangling labyrinthine maze
   Of doctrine, creed, and theory; from vague
  Vain speculations; the detested plague
Of spiritual pride, and vile affrays
  Sectarian, good Lord, deliver me!
Nature! thy placid monitory glory
Shines uninterrogated, while the story
Goes round of this and that theology,
  This creed, and that, till patience close the list.
Once more on Carronben's wind-shrilling height
To sit in sovereign solitude, and quite
  Forget the hollow world—a pantheist
Beyond Bonaventura! This were cheer
Passing the tedious tale of shallow pulpiteer.

IX.

A VALE of tears, a wilderness of woe,
    A sad unmeaning mystery of strife;
Reason with Passion strives, and Feeling ever
Battles with Conscience, clear eyed arbiter.
    Thus spake I in sad mood not long ago,
To my dear father, of this human life,
    Its jars and phantasies. Soft answered he,
With soul of love strong as a mountain river:
    We make ourselves—Son, you are what you are
Neither by fate nor providence nor cause
    External: all unformed humanity
Waiteth the stamp of individual laws;
    And as you love and act, the plastic spirit
    Doth the impression evermore inherit.

X.

LAST Autumn we were four, and travelled far
  With Phœbe in her golden plenilune,
O'er stubble-fields where sheaves of harvest boon
Stood slanted. Many a clear and stedfast star
  Twinkled its radiance thro' crisp-leaved beeches,
Over the farm to which, with snatches rare
  Of ancient ballads, songs, and saucy speeches,
He hurried, happy mad. Then each had there
  A dove-eyed sister pining for him, four
Fair ladies legacied with loveliness,
  Chaste as a group of stars, or lilies blown
In rural nunnery. O God! Thy sore
  Strange ways expound. Two to the grave have
    gone
Without apparent reason more or less.

XI.

Now, while the long-delaying ash assumes
    The delicate April green, and, loud and clear,
Through the cool, yellow, mellow twilight glooms,
    The thrush's song enchants the captive ear;
Now, while a shower is pleasant in the falling,
    Stirring the still perfume that wakes around;
Now, that doves mourn, and from the distance calling,
    The cuckoo answers, with a sovereign sound,—
Come, with thy native heart, O true and tried!
    But leave all books; for what with converse high,
Flavoured with Attic wit, the time shall glide
    On smoothly, as a river floweth by,
Or as on stately pinion, through the grey
Evening, the culver cuts his liquid way.

XII.

WHY are all fair things at their death the fairest
    Beauty the beautifullest in decay?
Why doth rich sunset clothe each closing day
With ever-new apparelling the rarest?
    Why are the sweetest melodies all born
Of pain and sorrow? Mourneth not the dove,
In the green forest gloom, an absent love?
    Leaning her breast against that cruel thorn,
Doth not the nightingale, poor bird, complain
    And integrate her uncontrollable woe
To such perfection, that to hear is pain?
    Thus, Sorrow and Death—alone realities—
Sweeten their ministration, and bestow
    On troublous life a relish of the skies!

XIII.

AND, well-belovëd, is this all, this all?
    Gone, like a vapour which the potent morn
Kills, and in killing glorifies! I call
    Through the lone night for thee, my dear first-
        born
Soul-fellow! but my heart vibrates in vain.
    Ah! well I know, and often fancy forms
The weather-blown churchyard where thou art lain—
    The churchyard whistling to the frequent storms.
But down the valley, by the river side,
    Huge walnut-trees—bronze-foliaged, motionless
As leaves of metal—in their shadows hide
    Warm nests, low music, and true tenderness.
But thou, betrothed! art far from me, from me.
O heart! be merciful—I loved him utterly.

XIV.

FATHER! when I have passed, with deathly swoon,
Into the ghost-world, immaterial, dim,
O may nor time nor circumstance dislimn
My image from thy memory, as noon
Steals from the fainting bloom the cooling dew!
Like flower, itself completing bud and bell,
In lonely thicket, be thy sorrow true,
And in expression secret. Worse than hell
To see the grave hypocrisy—to hear
The crocodilian sighs of summer friends
Outraging grief's assuasive, holy ends!
But thou art faithful, father, and sincere;
And in thy brain the love of me shall dwell
Like the memorial music in the curved sea-shell.

XV.

FROM my sick-bed gazing upon the west,
    Where all the bright effulgencies of day
  Lay steeped in sunless vapours, raw and gray,—
Herein (methought) is mournfully exprest
    The end of false ambitions, sullen doom
Of my brave hopes, Promethean desires:
Barren and perfumeless, my name expires
    Like summer-day setting in joyless gloom.
Yet faint I not in sceptical dismay,
    Upheld by the belief that all pure thought
  Is deathless, perfect: that the truths out-wrought
By the laborious mind cannot decay,
    Being evolutions of that Sovereign Mind
    Akin to man's; yet orbed, exhaustless, undefined.

XVI.

THE daisy-flower is to the summer sweet,
    Though utterly unknown it live and die;
The spheral harmony were incomplete
    Did the dew'd laverock mount no more the sky,
    Because her music's linkëd sorcery
Bewitched no mortal heart to heavenly mood.
    This is the law of nature, that the deed
Should dedicate its excellence to God,
    And in so doing find sufficient meed.
Then why should I make these heart-burning cries,
    In sickly rhyme with morbid feeling rife,
For fame and temporal felicities?
Forgetting that in holy labour lies
    The scholarship severe of human life.

XVII.

O GOD, it is a terrible thing to die
  Into the inextinguishable life;
To leave this known world with a feeble cry,
  All its poor jarring and ignoble strife.
O that some shadowy spectre would disclose
  The Future, and the soul's confineless hunger
Satisfy with some knowledge of repose!
  For here the lust of avarice waxeth stronger,
Making life hateful; youth alone is true,
  Full of a glorious self-forgetfulness:
Better to die inhabiting the new
  Kingdom of faith and promise, and confess,
Even in the agony and last eclipse,
Some revelation of the Apocalypse!

XVIII.

WISE in his day that heathen emperor,
    To whom, each morrow, came a slave, and
        cried—
" Philip, remember thou must die ; " no more.
    To me such daily voice were misapplied—
Disease guests with me ; and each cough, or cramp,
    Or aching, like the Macedonian slave,
Is my *memento mori*. 'Tis the stamp
    Of God's true life to be in dying brave.
" I fear not death, but dying "*—not the long
    Hereafter, sweetened by immortal love ;
But the quick, terrible last breath—the strong
    Convulsion. Oh, my Lord of breath above !
Grant me a quiet end, in easeful rest—
A sweet removal, on my mother's breast.

---

* This is a saying of Socrates.

XIX.

OCTOBER'S gold is dim—the forests rot,
    The weary rain falls ceaseless, while the day
  Is wrapp'd in damp. In mire of village way
The hedge-row leaves are stamp'd, and, all forgot,
The broodless nest sits visible in the thorn.
  Autumn, among her drooping marigolds,
    Weeps all her garnered sheaves, and empty folds,
And dripping orchards—plundered and forlorn.
The season is a dead one, and I die!
  No more, no more for me the spring shall make
    A resurrection in the earth and take
The death from out her heart—O God, I die!
The cold throat-mist creeps nearer, till I breathe
Corruption. Drop, stark night, upon my death!

XX.

DIE down, O dismal day! and let me live.
    And come, blue deeps! magnificently strewn
With coloured clouds—large, light, and fugitive—
    By upper winds through pompous motions blown.
Now it is death in life—a vapour dense
    Creeps round my window till I cannot see
The far snow-shining mountains, and the glens
    Shagging the mountain-tops. O God! make free
This barren, shackled earth, so deadly cold—
    Breathe gently forth Thy spring, till winter flies
In rude amazement, fearful and yet bold,
    While she performs her custom'd charities.
I weigh the loaded hours till life is bare—
O God! for one clear day, a snowdrop, and sweet air!

XXI.

SOMETIMES, when sunshine and blue sky prevail—
    When spent winds sleep, and, from the budding larch,
Small birds, with incomplete, vague sweetness, hail
    The unconfirmed, yet quickening life of March,—
Then say I to myself, half-eased of care,
    Toying with hope as with a maiden's token—
"This glorious, invisible fresh air
    Will clear my blood till the disease be broken."
But slowly, from the wild and infinite west,
    Up-sails a cloud, full-charged with bitter sleet.
The omen gives my spirit deep unrest;
    I fling aside the hope, as indiscreet—
A false enchantment, treacherous and fair—
And sink into my habit of despair.

XXII.

O WINTER! wilt thou never, never go?
   O Summer! but I weary for thy coming;
Longing once more to hear the Luggie flow,
   And frugal bees laboriously humming.
Now, the east wind diseases the infirm,
   And I must crouch in corners from rough weather.
Sometimes a winter sunset is a charm—
   When the fired clouds, compacted, blaze together,
And the large sun dips, red, behind the hills.
   I, from my window, can behold this pleasure;
And the eternal moon, what time she fills
   Her orb with argent, treading a soft measure,
With queenly motion of a bridal mood,
Through the white spaces of infinitude.

XXIII.

OH, beautiful moon! Oh, beautiful moon! again
    Thou persecutest me until I bend
My brow, and soothe the aching of my brain.
    I cannot see what handmaidens attend
Thy silver passage as the heaven clears;
    For, like a slender mist, a sweet vexation
Works in my heart, till the impulsive tears
    Confess the bitter pain of adoration.
Oh, too, too beautiful moon! lift the white shell
    Of thy soft splendour through the shining air!
I own the magic power, the witching spell,
    And, blinded by thy beauty, call thee fair!
Alas! not often now thy silver horn
Shall me delight with dreams and mystic love forlorn!

XXIV.

'TIS April, yet the wind retains its tooth.
   I cannot venture in the biting air,
But sit and feign wild trash, and dreams uncouth,
   "Stretched on the rack of a too easy chair."
And when the day has howled itself to sleep,
   The lamp is lighted in my little room;
And lowly, as the tender lapwings creep,
   Comes my own mother, with her love's perfume.
O living sons with living mothers! learn
   Their worth, and use them gently, with no chiding
For youth, I know, is quick; of temper stern
   Sometimes; and apt to blunder without guiding.
So was I long, but now I see her move,
Transfigured in the radiant mist of love.

XXV.

LYING awake at holy eventide,
    While in clear mournfulness the throstle's hymn
Hushes the night, and the great west, grown dim,
Laments the sunset's evanescent pride:
Lo! I behold an orb of silver brightly
    Grow from the fringe of sunset, like a dream
From Thought's severe infinitude, and nightly
    Show forth God's glory in its sacred gleam.
Ah, Hesper! maidenliest star that ere
Twinkled in firmament! cool gloaming's prime
    Cheerer, whose fairness maketh wondrous fair
    Old pastorals, and the Spenserian rhyme:—
Thy soft seduction doth my soul enthral
Like music, with a dying, dying fall!

XXVI.

THERE are three bonnie Scottish melodies,
   So native to the music of my soul,
That of its humours they seem prophecies.
   The ravishment of Chaucer was less whole,
Less perfect, when the April nightingale
   Let itself in upon him. Surely, Lord!
Before whom psaltery and clarichord,
Concentual with saintly song, prevail,
   There lurks some subtle sorcery, to Thee
And heaven akin, in each woe-burning air!
   Land of the Leal, and *Bonnie Bessie Lee*,
And *Home, sweet Home*, the lilt of love's despair.
   Now, in remembrance even, the feelings speak,
   For lo! a shower of grace is on my cheek.

XXVII.

> "Thou art wearin' awa', Jean,
> Like snaw when it's thaw, Jean;
> Thou art wearin' awa'
> To the land o' the leal."

O THE impassable sorrow, mother mine!
   Of the sweet, mournful air which, clear and well,
For me thou singest! Never the divine
   Mahomedan harper, famous Israfel,
Such rich enchanting luxury of woe
   Elicited from all his golden strings!
Therefore, dear singer sad! chant clear, and low,
   And lovingly, the bard's imaginings,
O poet unknown! conning thy verses o'er
   In lone, dim places, sorrowfully sweet;
And O musician! touching the quick core
   Of pity, when thy skilful closes meet—
My tears confess your witchery as they flow,
Since I, too, *wear* away like the unenduring snow.

XXVIII.

UPLIFT in unparticipated night
    Oh indefinable Being! far retired
From mortal ken in uncreated light:
    While demonstrating glories unacquired
When shall the wavering sciences evolve
    The infinite secret, Thee? What mind shall scan
The tenour of Thy workmanship, or solve
    The dark, perplexing destiny of man?
Oh! in the hereafter border-land of wonder,
    Shall the proud world's inveterate tale be told,
The curtain of all mysteries torn asunder,
    The cerements from the living soul unrolled?
Impatient questioner, soon, soon shall death
Reveal to thee these dim phantasmata of faith.

XXIX.

AND thus proceeds the mode of human life
    From mystery to mystery again;
From God to God, thro' grandeur, grief, and strife,
    A hurried plunge into the dark inane
Whence we had lately sprung. And is't for ever?
    Ah! sense is blind beyond the gaping clay,
And all the eyes of faith can see it never.
    We know the bright-haired sun will bring the day,
Like glorious book of silent prophecy;
    Majestic night assume her starry throne;
The wondrous seasons come and go: but we
    Die, unto mortal ken for ever gone.
Who shall pry further? who shall kindle light
    In the dread bosom of the infinite?

XXX.

O THOU of purer eyes than to behold
    Uncleanness! sift my soul, removing all
  Strange thoughts, imaginings fantastical,
Iniquitous allurements manifold.
Make it into a spiritual ark; abode
    Severely sacred, perfumed, sanctified,
  Werein the Prince of Purities may abide—
The holy and eternal Spirit of God.
  The gross, adhesive loathsomeness of sin,
Give me to see. Yet, O far more, far more,
That beautiful purity which the saints adore
    In a consummate Paradise within
The Veil,—O Lord, upon my soul bestow,
An earnest of that purity here below.

Miscellaneous Poems.

A Winter Ramble.

JOHN Frost, old Nature's jeweller, had beautified the leas,
And the lustre of his fret-work was twinkling on the trees,
As we ramble o'er the meadows in a meditative ease.

We had left the town behind us for a roaming holiday,
Beneath an arc of gloom, all dark and indistinct it lay,

And the fog was wreathed about it like a robe of iron-gray.

But a carpeting of leaflets, and a canopy of blue,
And the mystery of ether as the warming sunshine grew,
Sent a mellow thrill of happiness our eager spirits through.

And over lanes, where Winter bluff had shook his hoary beard,
Where in the naked hedgerows the broodless nests appear'd,
And the brown leaves of the beech-tree were with silver gloss veneer'd.

We wandered and we pondered till half the morn was spent,
And the red orb through the tangled boughs his cunning vigour sent,

And the valley mists all melted at his glance omnipotent.

Dim on a sloping hill-side, clothed in a misty pall,
Stands a turret grey and hoary, where the ancient ivies crawl,
Their Arab arms round casement, sill, and door, and mould'ring wall.

And there we halted half-an-hour within a roofless hall,
'Neath a bower of wildest ivy hanging downwards from the wall,
Bearing in its grand luxuriance a flower funereal.

There we talked of the gay plumes erst bent to pass the lintel old,
The maidens that were moved to smile at gallant wooers bold,

The jovial nights of brave carouse, the wine-cups manifold.

And all the faded glories of the mediæval time,
When the age was in its manhood, and the land was in its prime,
And manly deeds were chanted in a bold heroic rhyme.

Then, plucking each a sprig, bedecked with simple yellow flower,
We scrambled sadly downwards from our old enchanted bower,
And the glory of the sunshine fell upon us like a shower.

Once more beneath the concave of a clear effulgent sky,
Where flocks of cawing rooks to the mansion wavered by—
A mansion standing coldly 'mid a windy rookery,

And over breezy mountains, where the poacher, with his gun,
Stood lonely as a boulder-stone 'tween earth and shining sun,
We wandered and we pondered till the winter day was done.

The Home-Comer.

OH, many a leaf will fall to-night,
　　As she wanders through the wood!
And many an angry gust will break
The dreary solitude.
I wonder if she's past the bridge,
Where Luggie moans beneath;
While rain-drops clash in slanted lines
On rivulet and heath.
Disease hath laid his palsied palm
Upon my aching brow;

THE HOME-COMER.

The headlong blood of twenty-one
Is thin and sluggish now.
'Tis nearly ten! A fearful night,
Without a single star
To light the shadow on her soul
With sparkle from afar:
The moon is canopied with clouds,
And her burden it is sore;—
What would wee Jackie do, if he
Should never see her more?
Aye, light the lamp, and hang it up
At the window fair and free;
'Twill be a beacon on the hill
To let your mother see.
And trim it well, my little Ann,
For the night is wet and cold,
And you know the weary, winding way
Across the miry wold.
All drenched will be her simple gown,

And the wet will reach her skin:
I wish that I could wander down,
And the red quarry win—
To take the burden from her back,
And place it upon mine;
With words of kind condolence,
To bid her not repine.

You have a kindly mother, dears,
As ever bore a child,
And heaven knows I love her well
In passion undefiled.
Ah me! I never thought that she
Would brave a night like this,
While I sat weaving by the fire
A web of phantasies.
How the winds beat this home of ours
With arrow-falls of rain;
This lonely home upon the hill
They beat with might and main.

And 'mid the tempest one lone heart
Anticipates the glow,
Whence, all her weary journey done,
Shall happy welcome flow.
'Tis after ten! Oh, were she here,
Young man altho' I be,
I could fall down upon her neck,
And weep right gushingly!
I have not loved her half enough,
The dear old toiling one,
The silent watcher by my bed,
In shadow or in sun.

My Brown Little Brother of Three.

> "Happy child!
> Thou art so exquisitely wild,
> I think of thee with many tears,
> For what may be thy lot in future years."
>
> WORDSWORTH.

THE goldening peach on the orchard wall,
   Soft feeding in the sun,
Hath never so downy and rosy a cheek
As this laughing little one.
The brook that murmurs and dimples alone
Through glen, and grove, and lea,
Hath never a life so merry and true
As my brown little brother of three.

From flower to flower, and from bower to bower,
In my mother's garden green,
A-peering at this, and a-cheering at that,
The funniest ever was seen ;—
Now throwing himself in his mother's lap,
With his cheek upon her breast,
He tells his wonderful travels, forsooth !
And chatters himself to rest.

And what may become of that brother of mine,
Asleep in his mother's bosom?
Will the wee rosy bud of his being, at last
Into a wild flower blossom?
Will the hopes that are deepening as silent and fair
As the azure about his eye,
Be told in glory and motherly pride,
Or answered with a sigh?

Let the curtain rest: for, alas! 'tis told
That Mercy's hand benign
Hath woven and spun the gossamer thread

That forms the fabric fine.
Then dream, dearest Jackie! thy sinless dream,
And waken as blythe and as free;
There's many a change in twenty long years,
My brown little brother of three.

The "Auld Aisle"—a Burying-Ground.

THIS is my last and farewell place on earth,
  In this unlevel square of soft green-sward.
I love it well. Beneath no trailing vine,
No prairie grass, no moaning yew tree's shade,
Within no hollow hard sarcophagus,
No barrëd tomb, I hope *I* e'er shall lie;
But, happed with daisy-mingled grass, where oft,
On Sabbath eve, when everything is still,
And every little glen within itself
Is heard to chaunt its masses o'er the sun,

Already shrouded with his blood-stained robes,
Some mindful ones will drop a ready tear
To nurture a white daisy, and will breathe
A gushing prayer of sighs to him below.
I shall not feel their footsteps over *me;*
I shall not hear their long-known voices speak;
For I'll be dead. Oh! dead! and yet why weep?
Oh! earthly hearts are weak to think of death!
And 'tis a cutting thought to see our hopes
All shivered like a bunch of autumn leaves,
And sunset games, and love—delightful love—
All buried in a grave. Yet it *must* come.

The wreck of centuries is buried here;
The very monuments are hoar with age;
The empty tower that sentinels them all
Wails when the gusts wild wander o'er the earth,
And creaks the rusty gate with careless Time.

Methinks I see the silent funeral
Wend slowly up this hill with soulless load.
Backward swings sullen the disusëd gate,
And quiet, with measured steps, they enter here,
And cross the moundy sward, amongst the stones,
To where the red clay gapes.   How mournfully
Are the last rites paid to a fleshly frame !
Behold the old man with the sunken eyes
And broken heart.   This was his eldest-born.
A black-eyed boy he was, and in his youth
He was his joy and hope.   And oft he gazed
Into his laughing face, and dreamed of times
When in *his* youthful strength he would *him* shield,
And help him to the stone before the door
In summer time, when streamlets murmured clear.
So he grew up, but scorned the homely ways
Of the grey place of his nativity.
He saw the sun rise from behind the hills,
His well-thumbed book firm clasped in his young hand.

He saw it sink within the breezy glen,
And all the birds shrink from its burning face
To shade in nests, his book firm clasped in hand.
But most he pondered over nature's book—
The bubbled rill and the green-bladed corn,
The lowly wild-flowers and the leafy trees
Alive with music. His father wondered strange,
And prouder grew of his bold quiet son,
Who spoke without restraint or lowly eye
Unto God's minister. And he would tell
At other fire-sides of his wondrous ways,
The oft-trimmed lamp when others were indrawn;
Nor did he check the working of the mind
And wearing of the flesh. *He* knew no harm.
So time grew older still, and he went off,
With paler face and heavier looks, to where
The sons of learning prosecute their toils.

But here he pined like a transplanted flower

Borne from its native soil. No grass was here,
Where he might lie, and watch the mighty clouds
All floating in the blue. No lark was here,
In love with angels, but the place was lone
And dark and cold. No milkmaid's song was here,
Hushed when he passed upon the mountain side,
And anxious eye that gazed till he was gone.
And 'mid the throng of battling human kind,
No simple eye nor horny hand sought his,
Or voice, with homely accents, spoke relief.
All was unknown, unheeded, but his books,
Which were his very self, his only friend.

And rich he was in lore, and strong in hope,
But heaven was panting for an inmate more:
In heaven his place was vacant; as at home.
And time grew older still, and he came home
To see his father, but he ne'er went back.
His body could not hold his restless soul,

That longed, with eagle strength, to pierce the clouds,
And so it burst this yielding bond on earth,
Already, by a lengthened struggle, weak.
His father saw him die. He never left
His bedside; but with eyes that seemed as glazed,
For ever staring at the sharpened face,
He stood and stood and wept not. In that time
His son saw heaven and chided all delay.
His father knew not of the words of blame
That blest his dying breath. He seized the clay,
And clutched it desperately unto his breast.
The arms fell down, nor gave returning press.
And that crush broke the doting father's heart.
This is the grave beside that white gravestone :
Hold back the nettles while I read its lay :—

Epitaph.

Beneath me lies the rotting faded mask
  Of a young mind that studied heaven well;

THE "AULD AISLE."

Ne'er in the sun of pleasure did he bask,
  But loved hope's shadow and fair virtue's dell.
He died while on the road to yonder sky,
  And every one that wanders careless here,
Tread soft, and hark! Is not time hurrying by?
  Begone and pray; the Day of Judgment's near!

I have seen children playing in this place,
Have heard the voice of psalms sound plaintive here,
And sighs commingle with these strains of love,
For memory is dewy with salt tears.

Yet some lie here unknown to all. They came
Parentless, and they died and buried were
By careless hands, that threw the wormy clods
All hastily upon the coffin lid
And then went home. Perhaps some empty chair,
Like to a last year's nest, still waits for them.
Perhaps a nightly prayer still ascends

Among the breathings of a family home,
To hasten their return. Let us away
And gather stones and place them at their heads.

Could all the tales that wait around the graves,
Like volumes of wet sighs, be garnered up:
How hollow would each swelling heap resound.

Here one who died in mirth, and while the laugh,
The merry laugh of joy did paint his face,
Death frowned, and smote the smiling victim dead.

Here one who wept to see the flushing sun
Glide reddening from his window bars, and set
To rise again, and dry the silent dew
From his damp grave.

     Here one who lingered long,
And every morn the fields missed knots of flowers

Borne to his bedside. And his eyes grew wild
When the sun's withering gaze stared in upon them,
And he would press them to his fluttering heart,
And face the mighty orb, defiant-like,
As if to hurl it from the empty sky,
For daring thus to blight his darling flowers.
Poor fellow, he was mad.

        May God forbid
That clownish foot should crush the gentle clay,
Or break the daisy stalks or primrose buds,
That bloom beside the low white marble stone
In yon lone spot.

To Jeanette.

> " I did hear you talk
> Far above singing; after you were gone,
> I grew acquainted with my heart, and searched
> What stirred it so! Alas! I found it love."

I'VE sung of flowers in loving way,
    And pluck'd them too for half a day,
And into posies wrought them, till
Orion glared above the hill:
But never, never saw I one
As fair as thee beneath the sun,
And never, never shall I know
A lovelier where'er I go.

TO JEANETTE.

Yet 'tis not for thy beauty, dear
Jeanette, nor yet the sunny cheer
About thy face, I love thee so!
But something of thy soul doth flow
Into my heart, and I am wild
With tender passion as a child.

I write thy name, and kiss it, dear
Jeanette, in most impulsive fear!
I whisper it into my heart,
And then its music makes me start
In sudden gladness. I am fain
To let the echo die again!
Thy image groweth out of air
Until, entranced, I pause and stare
Into thy dear ideal eyes—
The shadow of God's paradise.

I am in love with thee, thou dear

Jeanette, and keep my spirit clear
For thy embrace. It cannot be
That thou wilt keep aloof from me
Like that immortal Florentine
Whom Tasso lov'd. O I would pine
Into a pale accusing dream
To haunt thy pillow, and would seem
So fond and sad, thy heart would fret
For its unkindness, good Jeanette!

O many a long glad summer day
I laughed at love, and deemed his sway
The tinkle of an idle tongue,
A fancy only to be sung.
But thou all-beautiful! hast more
Of this, the thrilling passion—love—
In one soft tress of plaited gold,
Than blessed Petrarch could unfold.

TO JEANETTE.

I love thee, dear Jeanette! I love
Thee, O how dearly! Far above
All singing is my love for thee,
Thou paradise of ecstasy!
Make me immortal with a kiss
Of earnest pressure, and all bliss
Is mine for ever, ever! Dear
Jeanette, beloved, adored in fear!

The Poet and his Friend.

I SPENT a day—the landmark of a life—
    With one, a hero in the realms of rhyme:
Ardent, yet calm—in human wisdoms rife,
    And burning to be something in his time.
Through autumn foliage by a river side,
    Through glen of ivied trees and hazel dell,
Each heart by its own sunshine glorified,
    We wandered wildly wise; till it befel,
        Beneath a faded elm, we came upon a well.

And, sitting by the still translucent water,
  In pleasaunce sweet we quaffed the liquid cold;
Lo! as we drank, there passed a fairer daughter
  Of Beauty than Fidessa. Then the old—
Yet never old, immortal song of glory,
  Breathing of summer bower and emerald lea,
And fountain bubbling coldly—Spenser's story
  Thrilled all our brains to living ecstasy:
  Such power had maiden floating onward maidenly.

And pondered we, above that placid wave,
  How we were thrown upon a colder day;
Yet, by the sword of Arthur! quite as brave,
  As wondrous willing for the haughty fray
As Arthegal and Guyon. So we rose
  And joined our hands in fervent heat, and swore
By old Renown's endeavours, and by those
  Who battled well and won, to dream no more,
  But through a sea of fears to struggle for the shore.

I think no good of him who takes his ease,
   As pigeon-livered in the human game
As Braggadocio: on the tranquil seas
   All ships sail nobly; but whoe'er is tame
To face the waves when fringed with windy spray,
   Is but a coward.   Let him live, then rot!
No man shall speak of him, no pilgrim lay
   A twist of wild-flowers on the common spot
   That marks his meagre dust—the poltroon is forgot.

But, good friend! we shall fight.   Even he who fails
   In a great cause is noble.   Time will show
The best and worst of it; and while it hails
   Some worthy Song-kings of the long-ago,
Perhaps our names will echo with the rest,
   And in no feebleness.   Meantime, oh fight!
In the thick hurry of the battle press'd,
   Clothed on with resolution, the soul's might—
   Be Hector or Achilles!—God defend the right!

The Two Streams.

O COOL the summer woods
   Of dear Gartshore, where bloom
Soft clouds of white anemones
Among their own perfume.
And clear the little brooklet,
Singing an endless lay,
Winding its nameless waters
Close by the white highway.
And here in sweet sensation,
And soul-uneasy swoon,

I've lain for many a golden
Hour of a summer noon.
The cushats *crooned* around me
Their murmuring amorous song;
And in a brooding drowsiness,
The echoes swooned along;
Till all the sweet sensations
Grew into utter pain,
And I was fain to wander
All sadly home again.
There have been brotherhoods in song,
And human friendships true;
There have been lovers unto death,
Yes, and right many too.
But never in the march of time,
And ne'er in mortal knowing,
From history or nobler rhyme,
Hath there been such constant flowing:
One from mountains far away,

THE TWO STREAMS.

One from glades of emerald shining,
Flowing, flowing evermore
For a delicate combining.
If upon a summer's day,
When the air is blue and bracing,
You for Merkland take your way,
Sweet uneasy fancies chasing;
You may see the famous grove—
If not famous, then most surely
Ripe for fame, which is but love—
Where they mingle most demurely.
Not in song and babbling play
Which no poet could unravel;
But in tender simple way,
On a bed of golden gravel.
Where I sit I see them now,—
Bothlin with her endless winding
From a mountain's purple brow,
Sacred contemplation finding;

In still nooks of shady rest,
Gleaming greenly 'neath the holly:
Youth, she says, is often blest
With a touch of melancholy.
Luggie from the orient fields
Wiser is, yet hath a beauty,
Which the snowy conscience yields
To the softened face of duty.
All she does bespeaks a grace,
Yet the grace hath that of sadness
We behold in many a face,
Where we had expected gladness.
But when Bothlin meets her there,
See the change to sudden glory!
Surely such another pair
Never met in classic story.
I could sing for half a day,
And my spirit never weary
Fashioning the vernal lay

With a linnet's impulse cheery.
But some night in leafy June,
You the place yourself may see;
When the light is in the moon,
Like the passion that's in me.

Evening.

THE evening now is still and calm,
   As if sad Eloïsa's soul
Had breathed a spiritual balm
   Throughout the softened whole.
Within the azure of the sky
   There shineth not a single star;
But in a soft serenity
   The Crescent cometh from afar.
In darker lines the firs that shade
   The house of Merkland round and round,

EVENING.

Come out, and from the fragrant glade
   No liquid notes resound :
I heard the birds this live-long day,
   In sweet unwrinkled blending,
As if this merry month of May
   Should never have an ending.

O could I utter thoughts that rise,
   O could I sing the tender
Softness of the summer skies,
   In all their virgin splendour!

O crescent Moon, like pearlëd bark
   To ferry souls to glory;
O silent deepening of the dark
   O'er vale and promontory!

Alas, that I should live, and be
   A churl in soul, while slowly
God makes the solemn eve, and breathes
   A calm thro' hearts unholy!

The Love-Tryst.

SEVEN sycamores of wondrous fairness, smooth,
    And mealy green of trunk, and murmurous
In multitudinous sun-twinkling leaves,
This valley grace. Three fairer than the rest,
Which in the silent worship of my heart
I fondly call the brothers of Bridgend,
O'er cottage floors when doors are wide for heat
And often on the face of cradled child,
Throw dusky shadows. And when lenient winds
Blow motion, the cool shadows flicker, and play
Upon the floors, and glimpse the countenance

Of the sweet baby, till the mother laughs,
And bending downward, kisses. But of all
The trees that ever tufted hill or vale,
That ever took the breeze or sheltered nest,
Or rung with flowing melody of birds,
The strangest and the dearest, best and first,
Waves audibly upon a windy hill
Above the Luggie. In the front of Spring,
When the first crocus gleams among the grass,
One half shines out full-leaved, the other bare:
And when the Autumn violet hath lost
Its fragrance, and the meadow-hay is mown,
One half shines out full-leaved, the other bare.
There are two trees, whose marriageable boughs
Twine, each with each, and throw a common shade,
A chestnut and an elm. The former opes
Its oily buds whene'er the teeming south
Breathes life and warm intenerating balm,
But fades in early Autumn; while supreme

In vigorous development, the elm
Full-foliaged glimmers till October's end.
At the twin roots and facing the rich west
A summer seat is rustically carved,
A sylvan shelter from the mid-day sun:
But nor in mid-day, nor when decent eve
Gather her purples have I rested there;
But when thro' crisp and fleecy clouds the moon
O'er the soft orient sheds a milder dawn,
Then tripping up the dewy lea, with step
Light as an antelope, a maiden came,
And all her radiance in my bosom laid;
And on this seat, while high among the leaves
Rain murmured, and the glory of the moon
Was dimmed, I whispered all my passion-tale.
Ah me, ah me! her silken hair down-slid,
Her smooth comb dropt among the grass, and both
Stooped searching, and her burning cheek met mine:
And starting suddenly upward, with her face

THE LOVE-TRYST.

Rosed to the beating temples, meek she gazed,
Half sad, and the blue languish of her eyes
Drooped tearful. And in madness and delight,
I with my left arm zoned her little waist,
And with my right hand smoothed the silken hair
From her fair brow, snow-cold; and, by the doves
That bill and coo in Venus' pearly car!
There was a touch of lips. Then creeping close
Into my bosom like a little thing
That was confused, she cradled pantingly.
Thus, while the rain was murmuring overhead,
And the out-passioned moon thro' vaporous gloom
Dipt queenly, whispered I my perilous tale.
Ah me, ah me! a tender answer came;
For with her softling finger-tips she touched
My hand, warm laid upon her heart, and pressed
A meek approval with averted face.
O poet-maker, darling love, sweet love,
Awakener of manhood, and the life

Of life. But let me not like talking fool
Prate all thy virgin whiteness, all thy sweet
Deliciousness, for thou art living yet!
And as the rose that opens to the sun
Its downy leaves, scents sweetest at the core,
So all thy loveliness is but the robe
That clothes a maiden chastity of soul.

O hasten, hasten down your azure road,
And darken all the golden zones of heaven,
Bright Sun, for I am weary for my love.

An Epistle to a Friend.

AH well-a-day, for human plans,
    And Fancy's bright creations,
With all the purple-wingéd brood
    Of young imaginations!
I've tried, this weary winter's day,
    All poignant cares to banish,
By quaffing goblets, rosy-brimm'd,
    Of dear poetic Rhenish.

Not all the sweets of Castaly—
    That river Heliconian,

Adorn'd with swans of queenly snow,
   Of ancient brood Strymonian;
Not all the maiden Muses nine,
   With tresses loosely flowing,
Could magnetise a single line,
   Or set my quill a-going;

Until I thought of thee, dear friend—
   Best loved, though long unheeded;
Then forth the virgin pages came,
   And quick my fingers speeded.
This very hour I'll make amends,
   This lonely hour quiescent,
When all the stars are in the blue,
   'Mid lustre irridescent.

And, from the slopes I know right well,
   All shagg'd with bending thistle,
The homeless wind comes with a swell,

And enters with a whistle;
Till brightlier glows the cosy fire,
And cheerier my bosom,
In thinking on the shivering woods,
And vales without a blossom.

You know the Luggie, natal stream!—
On earth to us none dearer—
Where Lady Luna, mirror'd, burns,
With all her handmaids near her.
The time may come when haughty Fame
With laurel shall console us;
Then we shall halo it with song
Till it outflow Pactolus!

The woods, the vales, the hawthorn dales,
The hoary hamlet Caurnie
Shall be of goodlier report
Than genius-hallowed Ferney.

And though I speak like boaster vain,
    I speak not without thinking;
Already on thy noble brow
    I see a chaplet twinkling!

Heaven knows! amid the march of Time
    I am a simple dreamer;
Can see more in the patient moon—
    Yon radiant crescent-gleamer—
Than all the banner'd pomp of war,
    Or progress politician;
Than all the mockeries of rank,
    And haughtiness patrician.

No golden key, however bright,
    Can pass the fragrant portal
Of Fame's grand temple-dome, or make
    A simpleton immortal.
Then what is wealth to our desire?

(A burning tear-drop pays us)
A rushlight to the morning star,
    To Homer but a Crœsus.

Then, Willie, though a careless dog,
    In brotherhood excuse me,
Nor with neglect, and haughty look,
    Most wantonly abuse me.
I've suffer'd much and suffer'd long,
    Dear heart! since last we ponder'd
On gentle love, within that hall
    Where ancient ivies wander'd.

Nor think my love one jot the less—
    Than love I sought in passion—
Because I thus have treated thee
    In unpoetic fashion.
Let this suffice for evermore:
    I plead a self-conviction,

And thy frank spirit never shall
    Increase my sad affliction.

Then sure I'll see thee yet again,
    Before another morrow
Steals up the east—shall see thee, friend!
    In a delightful sorrow.
With silent gratitude, I speak
    A blessing on our meeting,
And may the light of friendship touch
    Our spirits at the greeting!

A Vision of Venice.

BEHOLD! a waking vision crowns my soul
    With beatific radiance, and the light
Of shining hope;—a golden-memoried dream
That clings unto my youth, as clung the strange
Leonine phantom to that mystic man,
Lean Paracelsus. It has grown with me
Like destiny, or that which seems to be
My destiny, ambition: and its glow
Inflames my fancy, as if some clear star
Had burst in silvery light within my brain.
From the smooth hyaline of that far sea

The pictured Adriatic rises, fair
As dream, a kingly-built and tower'd town;
Column and arch and architrave instinct
With delicatest beauty; overwrought
With tracery of interlacèd leaves
For ever blooming on white marble, hush'd
In everlasting summer, windless, cold:
The city of the Doges!

      From the calm
Transparent waters float some thrilling sounds
Of Amphionic music, and the words
Are Tasso's, where he passions for his love,
That lady Florentine so lily-smooth,
Clothed on with haughtiness!

       At the black stair
Of palace rising shadowy from the wave,
Two singing gondolieri wait a freight

Of loveliness. A tremulous woman, robed
In dazzling satin, and whose dimpled arms,
And milky heaving breasts of living snow
Shine through their veil diaphanous, floats down
From the wide portal; and the ivory prow
Of the soft-cushion'd gondola (as she
Steps lightly from the marble to her place)
Dips, rises, dips again; then through the blue
Swift glides into the sunset.

       Oh, the glow
Of that rich sunset dims whate'er I see
In this my own dear valley! O'er the hills—
Those craggy Euganean hills, whose peaks
Wedge the clear crystalline—a blazonry
Of clouds pavilion'd, folded, interwound
Inextricably, load the breezeless west
With awe and glory. The effulgence gleams
Upon a vision'd Belmont, home of her
Who loved as Shakespeare's women do; and gleams

Upon those walls wherein Othello's spear
Stabb'd clinging innocence; where that poor wife,
The love-Cassandra Belvidera, gave
Her soul in martyrdom to love and woe.

And shall I never that far town behold,
Crested with sparkling columns, fiery towers,
Praxitelean masonry?—behold
VENICE, the mart of nations, ere I die?
By Heaven! her common merchants princes were
Unto the continents; her traffickers
The honourable of the earth! She stood
A crownèd city, and the fawning sea
Licked her white feet; and the eternal sun
Kissed with departing beam her brow of snow!

*   *   *   *   *   *

Woe to this Venice, with her crown of pride!
The Lady of the kingdoms, the perfection
Of beauty, and the joy of the whole earth!

Through her pavilions shall the crannying winds
Whistle, and all her borders in the sea
Crumble their Parian wonder. Woe to her,
Whose glorious beauty is a fading flower!
Her sober-suited nightingales, with notes
Of smooth liquidity and softened stops,
Solace the brakes; and 'mid her ancient streets
Tawny, the gleaming and harmonious sea
Makes silvery melody of bygone days.
O white Enchantment! Ocean-spouse of old!
When thy high battlements and bulging domes,
By sunset purpled, trembled in the wave!
Now o'er thy towers the Lord hath spread his hand,
And as a cottage shalt thou be removed;
Like Nineveh, or cloudy Babylon!

The Anemone.

I HAVE wandered far to-day,
  In a pleased unquiet way;
Over hill and songful hollow,
Vernal byeways, fresh and fair,
Did I simple fancies follow;
Till upon a hill-side bare,
Suddenly I chanced to see
A little white anemone.

Beneath a clump of furze it grew;
And never mortal eye did view

THE ANEMONE.

Its rathe and slender beauty, till
I saw it in no mocking mood;
For with its sweetness did it fill
To me the ample solitude.
A fond remembrance made me see
Strange light in the anemone.

One April day when I was seven,
Beneath the clear and deepening heaven,
My father, God preserve him! went
With me a Scottish mile and more;
And in a playful merriment
He deck'd my bonnet o'er and o'er—
To fling a sunshine on his ease—
With tenderest anemones.

Now, gentle reader, as I live,
This snowy little bloom did give
My being most endearing throes.

I saw my father in his prime;
But youth it comes, and youth it goes,
And he has spent his blithest time:
Yet dearer grown thro' all to me,
And dearer the anemone.

So with the spirit of a sage
I pluck'd it from its hermitage,
And placed it 'tween the sacred leaves
Of *Agnes' Eve* at that rare part
Where she her fragrant robe unweaves,
And with a gently beating heart,
In troubled bliss and balmy woe,
Lies down to dream of Porphyro.

Let others sing of that and this,
In war and science find their bliss;
Vainly they seek and will not find
The subtle lore that nature brings

Unto the reverential mind,

The pathos worn by common things,

By every flower that lights the lea,

And by the pale anemone.

The Yellowhammer.

IN fairy glen of Woodilee,
    One sunny summer morning,
I plucked a little birchen tree,
The spongy moss adorning;
And bearing it delighted home,
I planted it in garden loam,
Where, perfecting all duty,
It flowered in tassel'd beauty.

When delicate April in each dell
Was silently completing

THE YELLOWHAMMER.

Her ministry in bud and bell,
To grace the summer's meeting;
My birchen tree of glossy rind
Determined not to be behind;
So with a subtle power
The buds began to flower.

And I could watch from out my house
The twigs with leaflets thicken;
From glossy rind to twining boughs
The milky sap 'gan quicken.
And when the fragrant form was green
No fairer tree was to be seen,
All Gartshore woods adorning,
Where doves are always mourning.

But never dove with liquid wing,
Or neck of changeful gleaming,
Came near my garden tree to sing

Or *croodle* out its meaning.
But this sweet day, an hour ago,
A yellowhammer clear and low,
In love and tender pity
Thrilled out his dainty ditty.

And I was pleased, as you may think,
And blessed the little singer:
'O fly for your mate to Luggie brink,
Dear little bird! and bring her;
And build your nest among the boughs,
A sweet and cosy little house
Where ye may well content ye,
Since true love is so plenty.

And when she sits upon her nest,
Here are cool shades to shroud her.'
At this the singer sang his best,
O louder yet, and louder;

Until I shouted in my glee,
His song had so enchanted me.
No nightingale could pant on
In joy so wise and wanton.

But at my careless noise he flew,
And if he chance to bring her
A happy bride the summer thro'
'Mong birchen boughs to linger,
I'll sing to you in numbers high
A summer song that shall not die,
But keep in memory clearly
The bird I love so dearly.

The Cuckoo.

LAST night a vision was dispelled,
    Which I can never dream again;
A wonder from the earth has gone,
A passion from my brain.
I saw upon a budding ash
A cuckoo, and she blithely sung
To all the valleys round about,
While on a branch she swung.
Cuckoo, cuckoo! I looked around,
And like a dream fulfilled,

THE CUCKOO.

A slender bird of modest brown,
My sight with wonder thrilled.
I looked again and yet again;
My eyes, thought I, do sure deceive me,
But when belief made doubting vain,
Alas, the sight did grieve me.
For twice to-day I heard the cry,
The hollow cry of melting love;
And twice a tear bedimmed my eye—
I *saw* the singer in the grove,
I saw him pipe his eager tone,
Like any other common bird,
And, as I live, the sovereign cry
Was not the one I always heard.

O why within that lusty wood
Did I the fairy sight behold?
O why within that solitude
Was I thus blindly overbold?

My heart, forgive me! for indeed
I cannot speak my thrilling pain:
The wonder vanished from the earth,
The passion from my brain.

Fame.

A Fragment.

O GLORIOUS Fame! next grandest word to God,
    Father of all things beautiful and grand,
Of all the thoughts ideal and sublime
That grace the annals of our literature.
Thou stirrer of the heart to noble deeds!
Thou powerful antidote to cringing fear
Of battle, rolling 'mid the billowy smoke
That wreaths its curls blue over flood and field!
In the cold, creaking garret, or beside
The entrance to a theatre, or where

Luxury pillows soft the somnolent head,
Or where the dew-bent daisy droops to kiss
The dark grey eggs of lark, companion sweet!
There thou dost lift their souls above this world,
And teachest them in language fair and wild,
To ope their hearts in strains of poesy.
Ah, noble Fame! how deeply I adore
Thy altar, smelling sweet with fond applause!
Sages may shun, philosophers may scorn;
But, ah! to a young heart, how glorious
The thought that he, by well-earned merit, shall
Be spoken of, yea praised, 'neath the roof-tree
Of peasant, or beneath the monarch's dome!
That learned men will wonder, and in joy
Will lift their hands and shake astonished heads;
That by the fireside, while the flick'ring lamp
Doth send its shadow-forming light athwart.
The genius young shall read, and read, and read
Until the warning bell strike one short hour,

Then fling it past, and, pillowed on his couch,
Dream of the happy-gifted one that wrote it;
That maidens, high in rank and fair in form,
Shall speak to one another of that man
Who, bathing in the pure Castalian fount,
Arose, and from his form with pearlets clad
Shook off the diamonds in bright profusion,
That, while the clouds do tell their pattering beads,
And through the forest roars the wailing wind
Sporting with the brown leaves that wheel aloft,
A joyous family, seated by a fire
That roars in laughter at the storm without,
Talked of the poet——

Honeysuckle.

STOP! taste the balmy essence of this flower,
   That fondly twines about the dark-green fir;
The air is sweet, and, like a mild-eyed saint,
It liveth doing good. The balmy gale
Far wafts its odours to the lowly door
Of yon small cot thatched with the dying heath,
And the old dame doth bless the laden wind.
I do not think that e'er a tender eye
Looked on thee but with love,—that e'er a tongue
Spoke of thee but with blessings and with praise.

Thy lean red shanks cling round the dusty trunk,
And send their white shoots through the brown rough
    bark,
So true, so fond and frail-like that when one
Looks on thee, his mind's eye sees round God's
    throne
White spirits breathing hymns and fed with love.
Ye sweet, sweet flowers! ye must have mutual love,
For when one stalk, with its own beauty, droops,
With oily leaves and breathing blossoms heavy,
The others haste their sister to upraise,
And, winding round it with affection's grasp,
Lift it from off the earth's dark dreaded breast.
How many nosegays have I often culled
Of thee, fair guiltless thief, for even thy name
Tells how thou *sucklest* nature's *honeyed* sweets,
And leav'st her less wherewith to bless the rest.
Thou art not *very* beauteous; many flowers,
With high-fringed crests and gaudy-spotted leaves,

Outstrip thy homely dress; but tell me one
That blesseth ether with more fragrant smell?
'Tis ever thus. Furred robes and shining silks
Oft hide a poppy's smell—a dastard mind;
And homely garments oft adorn a breast
That heaves at pity's tale and tale of wrong,
And, known by none, yet is a friend to all.

Where the Lilies used to Spring.

WHEN the place was green with the shaky grass,
   And the windy trees were high;
When the leaflets told each other tales,
   And the stars were in the sky;
When the silent crows hid their ebon beaks
   Beneath their ruffled wing—
Then the fairies watered the glancing spot
   Where the lilies used to spring!

When the sun is high in the summer sky,
   And the lake is deep with clouds;

When gadflies bite the prancing kine,
    And light the lark enshrouds—
Then the butterfly, like a feather dropped
    From the tip of an angel's wing,
Floats wavering on to the glancing spot
    Where the lilies used to spring!

When the wheat is shorn and the burns run brown,
    And the moon shines clear at night;
When wains are heaped with rustling corn,
    And the swallows take their flight;
When the trees begin to cast their leaves,
    And the birds, new-feathered, sing—
Then comes the bee to the glancing spot
    Where the lilies used to spring!

When the sky is grey and the trees are bare,
    And the grass is long and brown,
And black moss clothes the soft damp thatch,

And the rain comes weary down,
And countless droplets on the pond
Their widening orbits ring—
Then bleak and cold is the silent spot
Where the lilies used to spring!

Snow.

FLOWERS upon the summer lea,
　　Daisies, kingcups, pale primroses—
These are sung from sea to sea,
As many a darling rhyme discloses.
Tangled wood and hawthorn dale
In many a songful snatch prevail;
But never yet, as well I mind,
In all their verses can I find
A simple tune, with quiet flow,
To match the falling of the snow.

SNOW.

O weary passed each winter day,
And windily howled each winter night;
O miry grew each village way,
And mists enfolded every height;
And ever on the window pane
A froward gust blew down with rain,
And day by day in tawny brown
The Luggie stream came heaving down:—
I could have fallen asleep and dreamed
Until again spring sunshine gleamed.

And what! said I, is this the mode
That Winter kings it now-a-days?
The Robin keeps its own abode,
And pipes his independent lays.
I've seen the day on Merkland hill,
That snow has fallen with a will,
Even in November! Now, alas;
The whole year round we see the grass:—

Ah, winter now may come and go
Without a single fall of snow.

It was the latest day but one
Of winter, as I questioned thus;
And sooth! an angry mood was on,
As at a thing most scandalous;—
When lo! some hailstones on the pane
With sudden tinkle rang amain,
Till in an ecstasy of joy
I clapp'd and shouted like a boy—
Oh, rain may come and rain may go,
But what can match the falling snow!

It draped the naked sycamore
On Foordcroft hill, above the well;
The elms of Rosebank o'er and o'er
Were silvered richly as it fell.
The distant Campsie peaks were lost,

And farthest Criftin with his host
Of gloomy pine-trees disappeared,
Nor even a lonely ridge upreared.—
Oh, rain may come and rain may go,
But what can match the falling snow!

Afar upon the Solsgirth moor,
Each heather sprig of withered brown
Is fringed with thread of silver pure
As slow the soft flakes waver down;
And on Glenconner's lonely path,
And Gartshore's still and open strath,
It falleth, quiet as the birth
Of morning o'er the quickening earth.—
Oh, rain may come and rain may go,
But what can match the falling snow!

And all around our Merkland home
Is laid a sheet of virgin lawn;

On fairer, softer, ne'er did roam
The nimble Oread or Faun.
There is a wonder in the air,
A living beauty everywhere;
As if the whole had ne'er been planned,
But touched by Merlin's famous wand,
Suddenly woke beneath his hand
To potent bliss in fairy show—
A mighty ravishment of snow!

October.

SWEET Muse and well-beloved, with my decline
  Declining, like a rose crushed unawares,
Having too early knowledge of decay,
Too subtle pleasure to behold the tree
Shed its thin foliage on the sluggish stream,—
What a sweet subject for thy silver sounds!

O for a quill pluck'd from the soaring wing
Of an archangel, dipped in holy dew,
To catch thy latest looks, thou loveliest
October, o'er the many-coloured woods!

October! vastlier disconsolate
Than Saturn guiding melancholy spheres,
Through ante-mundane silence and ripe death.
Ere the last stack is housed, and woods are bare,
And the vermilion fruitage of the brier
Is soaked in mist, or shrivelled up with frost;
Ere warm Spring nests are coldly to be seen
Tenantless, but for rain and the cold snow,
While yet there is a loveliness abroad,—
The frail and indescribable loveliness
Of a fair form Life with reluctance leaves,
Being there only powerful,—while the earth
Wears sackcloth in her great prophetic grief:—

Then the reflective melancholy soul,—
Aimlessly wandering with slow falling foot
The heath'ry solitude, in hope to assuage
The cunning humour of his malady,—
Loses his painful bitterness, and feels

His own specific sorrows one by one
Taken up in the huge dolour of all things.

O the sweet melancholy of the time
When gently, ere the heart appeals, the year
Shines in the fatal beauty of decay!
When the sun sinks enlarged on Carronben,
Nakedly visible without a cloud,
And faintly from the faint eternal blue
(That dim, sweet harebell-colour) comes the star
Which evening wears;—when Luggie flows in mist,
And in the cottage windows one by one,
With sudden twinkle household lamps are lit,
What noiseless falling of the faded leaf!

Sweet on a blossoming summer's afternoon,
When Fancy plays the wizard in the brain,
Idly to saunter thro' a lusty wood!
But sweeter far—by how much sweeter, God

Alone hath knowledge—in a pensive mood,
Outstretched on green moss-velvet floss'd with thyme,
To watch the fall o' the leaf before the moon
Shines out in sweet completion circular.
For when the sunset hath withdrawn its gold
And tawny glimmering, like the surcease
Of rich, low melody, erst inaudible streams
Find voices in their still unwearied flow;
And winds that have been much above the moors
And mountains, have a deadly feel of cold,
Forespeaking clear blue dawns and frosty chill.

The Roman Dyke.

AH! frail memorial of a thousand years!
Thou seem'st a stranger in a foreign land:
No pitying hand thy fragments, fall'n, uprears,
But useless, graceless, thou art left to stand.
And yet, across this foggy, rain-slash'd wall,
The savage tatoo'd Caledonians slew,
With gory club, the high-nosed Romans, who
With joy retreated at Antonius' call.
That stone which now I touch has handled been
By brawny Romans, who, in Latin talked

Of their fantastic foes, as, oft-times seen,
  With sacred tramp of liberty they stalked.
And have they e'er been slaves? that dyke shall tell:
  The Romans, Saxons, Southrons, Swedes, they've braved,
  And, like proud eagles, scorned to be enslaved;
As freemen now they stand—as freemen then they fell.
On that side scorn the paths of slavery;
Here—kiss the hallowed dust of Liberty!

Miscellaneous Sonnets.

Ezekiel.

EZEKIEL, thus from the Lord God: Behold,
    Mount Seir, I am against thee! Desolate,
Most desolate thy cloudy and dark fate.
Between the lips of talkers bad and bold,
Thy towns forsaken, and thy rivers rolled
    Thro' silent wastes, are taken up, and great
    The joy at thy high glories ruinate.
While all the earth is wanton, thou art cold,
    For thy most cruel lifting of the spear
'Gainst Israel in her time of consternation.
    Slain men shall fill thy mountains, O mount Seir!
Sith thou hast blood pursued, fell tribulation
    Shall curse thy blessings, mock'd and undeplored:—
    As I live, thou shalt know I am the Lord!

The Mavis.

SWEET Mavis! at this cool delicious hour
   Of gloaming, with a pensive quietness
Hushes the odorous air,—with what a power
   Of impulse unsubdued, thou dost express
Thyself a spirit! While the silver dew
   Holy as manna on the meadow falls,
Thy song's impassioned clarity, trembling through
   This omnipresent stillness, disenthrals
The soul to adoration. First I heard
   A low thick lubric gurgle, soft as love,
Yet sad as memory, thro' the silence poured
Like starlight. But the mood intenser grows,
   Precipitate rapture quickens, move on move
Lucidly linked together, till the close.

Despondency.

O MYSTERY of love and human grief,
   And hope, half-prophet ever prone to tears !
My heart is lonely as a withered leaf
Upon the winter tree. The passing years
Are barren to me of all happiness,
And, like a hoary anchorite, I feed
Upon my past, and, *fetisch-like*, it dress
With glory and clear jewels not its own.
O Love, and Childhood ! and those happy times
When ignorance was patron to my need,
When every hour was like a linnet flown
In song, and beautiful in simple rhymes.
Would that my feelings knew the quiet flow
Of thy clear waters, Luggie ! singing as they go !

The Moon.

I.

COME, light-foot Lady! from thy vaporous hall,
    And, with a silver-swim into the air,
Shine down the starry cressets one and all
    From Pleiades to golden Jupiter!
I see a growing tip of silver peep
    Above the full-fed cloud, and lo! with motion
Of queenly stateliness, and smooth as sleep,
    She glides into the blue for my devotion.
O sovran Beauty! standing here alone
    Under the insufferable infinite,
I worship with dazed eyes and feeble moan
    Thy lucid persecution of delight.
Come, cloudy dimness! Dip, fair dream, again!
O God! I cannot gaze, for utter pain.

The Moon.

II.

WITH what a calm serenity she smooths
    Her way thro' cloudless jasper sown with stars!
Chaster than virtue, sweeter than sweet truths
    Of maidenhood, in Spenser's knightly wars.
For what is all Belphœbe's golden hair,
    The chastity of Britomart, the love
Of Florimel so faithful and so fair,
    To thee, thou Wonder! And yet far above
Thy inoffensive beauty must I hold
    Dear Una, sighing for the Red-cross Knight
Thro' all her losses, crosses manifold.
    And when the lordly lion fell in fight,
Who, who can paragon her tearful woe?
Not thou, O Moon! didst ever passion so.

The Luggie.

I.

LONG yearnings had my soul to gaze upon
    Fair Italy with atmosphere of fire;
On tawny Spain; on th' immemorial land
Where Time has dallied with the Parthenon
    In beautiful affection and desire.
But when last even, effluently bland,
    I saw sweet Luggie wind her amber waters
Thro' lawns of dew and glens of glimmering green,
    And saw the comeliness of Scotland's daughters,
Their speaking eyes and modest mountain mien,—
    I blest the Godhead over all presiding,
Who placed me here, removed from human strife,
    Where Luggie, in her clear unwearied gliding,
Is but the image of my inner life.

The Luggie.

II.

THE Avon is a famous rivulet,
 The mountain Duddon and the "bonnie Doon"
Flow ever-shining in the sun of song,
While plaintive Yarrow moaneth evermore.
But there is one which I must halo yet
With verse, as with a gleam of morning glory;
Must set its woodland murmurings to tune,
As through summer groves it steals along;
Must gather inspiration from its love
Of visible beauty and traditions hoary,
And spiritual presences sublime.
Dear Luggie! thou are mine by right of birth,
And daily brotherhood and poet's rhyme.
O could I make thee famous o'er the earth!

The Luggie.

III.

PACTOLUS singeth over golden sand;
    Scamander, old and blood-empurpled river,
Rolls yet her stream divine; and Castaly
    Flows lucid in the light of ancient song;
Whilst thou, sweet Luggie! fairest of this land,
    And fair as any of that famous throng,
In pastoral, still loveliness, must be
    Bald as a marshy brooklet nameless ever!
Nay, by the spirit of beauty and dear pleasure,
    Sure I shall sing thee as my first delight,
Nurse of my soul, companion of my leisure!
    And if in aftertime thy waters roll
More worthily, more spiritually bright,
    It will be sunshine to my perfect soul.

Thomas the Rhymer.

LISTEN, O spirit of that ancient bard!
   Thou weird Ezekiel of an age of lies
And human fantasy! If 'neath the skies
One being liveth, worthy to be heard,
Whisper the awful *sesame* that unstarr'd
To thee the riddle of those mysteries,
Dumb evermore to gazing of all eyes
Mortal and uninspired! O thou that warr'd
With man and custom, I do think of thee
As something of a glory, something grand
Beyond what ever satisfied this land
With earnest of a strange divinity,
   Penn'd in thy passionately-breathing moods,
   Prophetic peopler of old solitudes!

The Lime-Tree.

A LIME-TREE broad of bough and rough of trunk
    Deepens a shadow, as the evening cool,
  Over the Luggie gathering in deep pool
Contemplative, its waters summer-shrunk;
The Lammas floods have sucked away the mould
    About its roots, and now in bare sunshine
    Like knot of snakes they twine and intertwine
Fantastic implication, fold in fold.
Secure in covert, 'neath the fringing fern
    Lurks the bright-speckled trout, untroubled, save
When boyhood with a glorious unconcern
    Eagerly plunges in the sleeping wave.
Here the much-musing poet might recapture
The inspiration flown, the vagrant rapture.

The Brooklet.

O DEEP unlovely brooklet, moaning slow
   Thro' moorish fen in utter loneliness!
The partridge cowers beside thy loamy flow
   In pulseful tremor, when with sudden press
The huntsman flusters thro' the rustled heather.
   In March thy sallow-buds from vermeil shells
Break, satin-tinted, downy as the feather
   Of moss-chat that among the purplish bells
Breasts into fresh new life her three unborn.
   The plover hovers o'er thee, uttering clear
And mournful—strange, his human cry forlorn:
   While wearily, alone, and void of cheer
Thou glid'st thy nameless waters from the fen,
To sleep unsunned in an untrampled glen.

Maidenhood.

A SACRED land, to common men unknown,
    A land of bowery glades and greenwoods hoary,
Still waters where white stars reflected shone,
    And ancient castles in their ivied glory.
Fair knights caparison'd in golden mail,
    And maidens whose enchantment was their beauty,
Met but to whisper each the passion-tale,
    For love was all their pleasure and their duty.
Here cedar bark, as with a moving will,
    Floated thro' liquid silver, all untended;
Here wrong and baseness ever came to ill,
    And virtue with delight was sweetly blended.
This land, dear Spenser! was thy fair creation,
Made thro' fine glamour of imagination.

Sleep.

O PRECIOUS Morphia! I sanctify
    The soothing power that in a painless swoon
Laps my weak limbs, giving me strength to lie,
    Till sacred dawn increases unto noon :
Then when, from highest meridional height,
    The sun devolves, and cooling breezes wake,
It is a comfort and divine delight
    The weary bed exhausted to forsake,
And bathe my temples in the blessed air.
    But when day wanes, and the wind-moaning night
Deepens to darkness, then thy virtue rare,
    O dream-creative liquid! brings delight,
Thy silver drops, diffusive, kindly steep
The senses in the golden juice of sleep.

The Days of Old Mythology.

O FOR the days of old Mythology,
    When dripping Naiads taught their streams to glide !
When, 'mid the greenery, one would oft-times spy
    An Oread tripping with her face aside.
The dismal realms of Dis by Virgil sung,
    Whose shade led Dante, in his virtue bold,
All the sad grief and agony among,
    O'er Acheron, that mournful river old,
Ev'n to the Stygian tide of purple gloom !
    Pan in the forest making melody !
And far away where hoariest billows boom,
    Old Neptune's steeds with snorting nostrils high !
These were the ancient days of sunny song ;
Their memory yet how dear to the poetic throng.

Discontentment.

O IF we never knew the genial hour
  When Happiness sits by us like a god
Dispensing treasures, we would never know
The barren sadness of the common day,
The weariness, and discontentment sour
At human life—its ordinary load
Of hopes deferred, and presences that flow
Smilingly past us, syrens in the dream
Of young imagination, fancy-fed.
O I have seen such beauties with the gleam
Of fairy sunshine on them, and I long
Upon their bosoms this my life away
To dally, like the lover in a song,
And be a luting swain, Arcadian bred!

Snow.

BUT yestermorn the February snow
　　Lay printless as the heaven upon this field,
And, with a rapture in my bosom born,
In sudden awe and reverence I kneeled
Alone beneath the glory of the sky
And omnipresent deity. To-day
The spirit of the beautiful no more
Over the wondering earth, in earnest glow
Touches to beauty all the landscape grey,—
Bringing a vision from her palace high
To this sublunar planet. Now, forlorn
As Ariadne on Cretan shore
For many bitter-cold and weary days
She knoweth not her old immortal ways.

The Thrush.

ONE Candlemas, a gentle day of Spring,
    I was abroad betimes while the red sun
Rose large and stately with a purpled ring
Of mist about him, and a mantle dun.
Thro' naked boughs he ominously glared,
Till, soul-constrained, in sudden awe I stood,
And with a Persian's adoration stared.
When lo! from a round beech-tree in the wood,
The only tree to which the brown leaves clung,
A mavis warbled forth his mellow lay;
And ever as his ditty clear he sung
The passion swelled his breast of downy grey.
Dear bird! since then thy melody I know
The boldest in intent, the fullest in its flow.

Stars.

O COLD blue night, and deep the cloudless sky
    Gleams, sown with lucid keen and trembling stars;—
A ravishment of glory shines on high,
And the rapt soul yearns upward. Fiery Mars
Shines with a baleful redness in the west;
While mail'd Orion, frozenly severe,
Stands like an armed skeleton opprest
With centuries of sentinelship. Thro' clear
Smooth ether the keen-silvered Plough upheaves
Its seven diamonds; and far away
Poor Cassiopeia for her daughter grieves—
Andromeda cold-touch'd by windy spray,
While faintly watching with tear-misted eyne,
Perseus flying shoreward o'er the gleaming brine.

My Epitaph.

*B*ELOW *lies one whose name was traced in sand.*
He died, not knowing what it was to live:
Died, while the first sweet consciousness of manhood
And maiden thought electrified his soul,
Faint beatings in the calyx of the rose.
Bewildered reader! pass without a sigh,
In a proud sorrow! There is life with God,
In other kingdom of a sweeter air;
In Eden every flower is blown: AMEN.

DAVID GRAY.

September 27, 1861.

Gray's Monument.

AT the inauguration of the Monument erected to the Poet's Memory in the "Auld Aisle" Burying Ground, Kirkintilloch, July 29, 1865, Mr. Bell said :—

David Gray, was born on the 29th January, 1838, and reared in his father's house here at Merkland till he reached his fourteenth year. His parents, seeing as they did his disposition and his genius, thought they might find means to bring up their son for the Church. With that view he was sent into Glasgow, and as he required funds to aid him in the prosecution of his studies, at that very early age he became a pupil-teacher in the city. He contrived also to attend the famous University there for four successive sessions. But during all that time his mind was brimming over with poetry, which rose like a rising tide above his Latin, above his Greek, above his theological studies. He had a very ardent and ambitious fancy; he had high aspirations; he had an earnest belief that he was born to be a poet, and to attain fame. In one so young it might have been thought that this was an overweening conception of his own powers. But in reality it was not. A poet is also a *vates* or prophet, and there is no reason why he should not be permitted sometimes to prophesy of himself. David Gray prophesied of himself that his name would yet be known to his fellow-countrymen as a poet and a teacher, for every true poet is a true teacher. In May, 1860, when he had so far completed his studies in Glasgow, and had arrived at the age of nearly 22, he started alone for London. He had read of the great literary world of the metropolis, and he was fired with an ambition to mingle in it and to make himself, if possible, known to some of the men there. He was fortunate in forming the acquaintance, very soon after going to London, of Mr. Monckton Milnes, now Lord Houghton, who at once formed a correct appreciation of the poet's character and genius. Lord Houghton has himself put it upon record that he found in David Gray what appeared to him to be the making of a great man. He has also recorded of him that upon first seeing him he was strongly reminded of the poet Shelley. Gray had a light, well-built form; he had a full brow and an out-looking eye; and he had a sensitive, melancholy mouth. So Lord Houghton speaks of him. He formed also in London other acquaintances of value, including Mr. Oliphant, then Private Secretary to Lord Elgin, now member for the Stirling Burghs. As to Sydney Dobell, the poet, I do not know that he actually formed the personal acquaintance of that gentleman; but he had frequent correspondence with Mr. Dobell, and received from him valuable letters, and suggestions, and assistance. He formed the acquaintance of a very estimable woman— Miss Marian James—herself an authoress of great reputation. Nearer at home he had already attained the friendly companionship of some whom he valued much. I am delighted to see two of those gentlemen present to-night —Mr. W. Freeland, David Gray's early and attached friend, now of the *Herald* Office, Glasgow, and Mr. James Hedderwick, himself a poet and an editor of great reputation. He had not, however, been long in London till he was seized with a cold which rapidly assumed the character of consumption. Lord Houghton and others, feeling deeply interested in him, got him sent to the South of England for a time; but the disease making rapid progress, David Gray was seized with an irresistible homesickness, and notwithstanding all the kindness, and all the attention of his friends in the South, in January, 1861, he made his re-appearance at his father's house down there in Merkland. He lived there from January, 1861, to the 3d December of the same year, when he died. That is the brief record of this young poet's life—almost all the incidents in it, all the events connected with it. But who can record, or who shall attempt to record the thousand thoughts and emotions that passed through his mind, that illuminated his fancy, and that kindled his genius? Who shall say how these familiar woods, and fields, and glens, and streams were to him dearer, a thousand times dearer and more romantic, than any woods, or fields, or glens, or streams in any other part of the world. No man but a true poet has that warm affection for home scenes, for his country, for his native land, for the friends of his youth; no man but a true poet has those sentiments in their height and in their depth; and if ever a man entertained them, the poetical remains of David Gray prove that he had them in a deep, pathetic, and most earnest manner. Upon his death-bed, within three days of his death, he received what appears to me to be a particularly beautiful letter from Marian James, breathing that *alma gentile* which none but a refined and pure woman possesses. I never saw David Gray, but I have seen to-night the humble room in which he was born; I have seen the home in which he was afterwards reared— a simple, rural house, belonging to a simple, honest, and upright family, such a family as Scotland is always proud of—and of such families I am proud to know that Scotland possesses her thousands and tens of thousands. I saw his mother to-night, and was deeply impressed with the apparent simplicity and earnestness of her character. I owe her my gratitude and my thanks for her presenting me with a book which belonged to her son, and which contains many of his private markings. I shall always retain it as a valuable and most esteemed possession. David Gray's poetical susceptibility was of the most conspicuous description. He had a most refined perception of the beautiful; he had a perception of an interminable vista of beauty and truth. He had noble and pure thoughts, and he has been enabled to express those noble and pure thoughts in very noble and pure language. "The Luggie" is a most remarkable poem, containing many very fine passages, inspired partially, no doubt, by a careful perusal of Thomson's "Seasons" and Wordsworth's "Excursion," and not, therefore, so entirely original as some of the author's subsequent poems; but with passages breaking out in it every now and then which neither Thomson nor Wordsworth suggested, and which are entirely the conceptions of David Gray's own genius. "The Luggie," as has been well said, "may not possess in itself much to attract the painter's eye, but it has sufficed for a poet's love." The series of sonnets entitled "In the Shadows"—written by the poet during his last illness— many of them bearing relation to his own condition, his own life, and his own prospects—appear to me to possess a solemn beauty not surpassed by many of the finest passages in Tennyson's "In Memoriam," totally distinct and unlike the "In Memoriam," but as genuine, as sincere, as heart-stirring, and often as poetical. In the author's own words, they admit you "to the chancel of a dying poet's mind;" you feel when you are reading these sonnets that they are written in the sure and immediate prospect of death; but they contain thoughts about life, about the past, and about the future, most powerful and most beautiful. I am not going to ask you to take all this for granted. I think, upon an occasion like this, we ought to show some little reason for the faith that is in us; and, if it will not fatigue you too much, I propose in a few minutes to read two or three of those passages and those sonnets which strike me as worthy of all admiration. I feel confident that these works are destined to take their place amongst standard poetical works in the library of every man of literary taste. We are here, as you have said, upon the occasion of the erection of a monument to David Gray—a monument erected on the spot where he is buried, in a beautiful old churchyard, standing upon the brow of a hill, from which a fine and extensive view of the surrounding valley and hills is commanded. It is a granite monument, and will last, I hope, for centuries. I am sure that in this neighbourhood it will often be visited by persons who feel something like kindred emotions with David Gray, and they will be proud of this neighbourhood that it gave birth in that humble cottage to a man who has added so much charm to its natural scenery. It was felt at the same time, I believe, by the gentlemen in Glasgow who took the principal charge of it, that a great or imposing monument was not the thing that was wanted. A plain, simple, enduring record of respect and esteem was what was wished. Therefore, although the fund I know could have been trebled, quadrupled, with ease, it was thought that when a certain moderate sum was obtained that was enough, and by the aid of the genius of our townsman, Mr. Mossman, I venture to say that an appropriate and suitable monument has now been erected on that spot. I may mention that I find the names in the list of subscribers very varied. Among the Glasgow subscribers I find the name of Mrs. Nichol, widow of the late Professor of Astronomy in our University, who I know took a great interest in David Gray from first to last, and who, I know also, with her usual benevolence, aided in smoothing his dying pillow. I find the name of William Logan, one of the most earnest and attached friends that David Gray ever had; I find Lord Houghton; I find Mr. Bailie Cochrane; I find Mr. Stirling of Keir, the Hon. Julia Fane, the Dowager Duchess of Sutherland, Mr. Macmillan, Mr. MacLehose, Mr. J. A. Campbell, Mr. Hutton, editor of the London *Spectator*, and many other names. Now Lord Houghton was requested to write an appropriate inscription for this monument. I know it was a labour of love with him, and I know he was anxious to write such an epitaph as would be thought suitable both here and elsewhere; and I venture to say, and I hope you will agree with me, that he has admirably succeeded in the simplicity and truth of that epitaph which has now been engraved on the monument. Such is the young man whose fame we shall not willingly let die, because they who read his works aright derive moral improvement and intellectual benefit from them—because, young as he was when he died, he cherished pure and noble thoughts, and because he has left those pure and noble thoughts as a record to us of his life, and as an incentive to us to endeavour to cherish similar thoughts. Therefore, we owe him a debt of gratitude; and, therefore, without attempting to raise him upon a pinnacle too high—for his life was cut short before the highest aims of his ambition were attained—let it go forth that no true poet in this land, be his position in life what it may, be his birth humble or great—no true poet, no great teacher of the hearts of men, will ever find an ungrateful country in Scotland, as long as it remembers its great poets—as long as it knows that it is the land of Burns. In "The Luggie," which you are aware is a descriptive and pastoral poem, there are varied moods of thought. There is a good deal of mere description of beautiful scenery, but that, whilst exquisitely done, is also intermingled with many thoughts and feelings which add a richness to the charm of the poet's description. No mere description of external and lifeless nature, unless brought home to the heart by allusions to human emotion, can ever produce a very strong effect. But David Gray seems to have understood admirably how to combine those two qualities in his descriptive picture, and whilst he describes beautiful external nature, he always takes care at the same time to attract and touch the feelings. I am happy to know that David Gray died in true Christian faith, and amity with all men. I know from the esteemed clergyman who attended him weekly for many a day, that he had those true Christian sentiments which become a man, and most of all become a great man, upon his death-bed. I have had the very greatest satisfaction in being present to-night. I felt it to be an honour to be requested to come here and express my sentiments on such a subject. It is an honour which I feel, and it is a pleasure which I feel still more, for when a man has passed through this world now for a good many years, as I have done, there can be nothing dearer to his heart than expressing sympathy with the great and good, and feeling those expressions of sympathy reflected from the hearts and the eyes of a sympathising audience.

The Monument bears the following inscription :—

THIS MONUMENT OF
AFFECTION, ADMIRATION, AND REGRET,
IS ERECTED TO
DAVID GRAY,
THE POET OF MERKLAND,
BY FRIENDS FROM FAR AND NEAR,
DESIROUS THAT HIS GRAVE SHOULD BE REMEMBERED
AMID THE SCENES OF HIS RARE GENIUS
AND EARLY DEATH,
AND BY THE LUGGIE, NOW NUMBERED WITH THE STREAMS
ILLUSTRIOUS IN SCOTTISH SONG.

Born 29th January, 1838; Died 3rd December, 1861.

www.ingramcontent.com/pod-product-compliance
Lightning Source LLC
Chambersburg PA
CBHW031816230426
43669CB00009B/1157